79,000 Steps

79,000 Steps is 44 photographs from
walks in New York City
(mostly mid to lower Manhattan)
during August 2022.

Published by Imaginary Dynamics
imaginarydynamics.com
ISBN: 978-1-971080-02-4

First Edition
File version 1 5 Z 362

There are no disclaimers, warranties, safety notices,
captions, or guarantees for this book or for anything in life.

79,000 Steps

Otto Kitsinger

Walks in New York City
(mostly mid to lower Manhattan)
during August 2022.

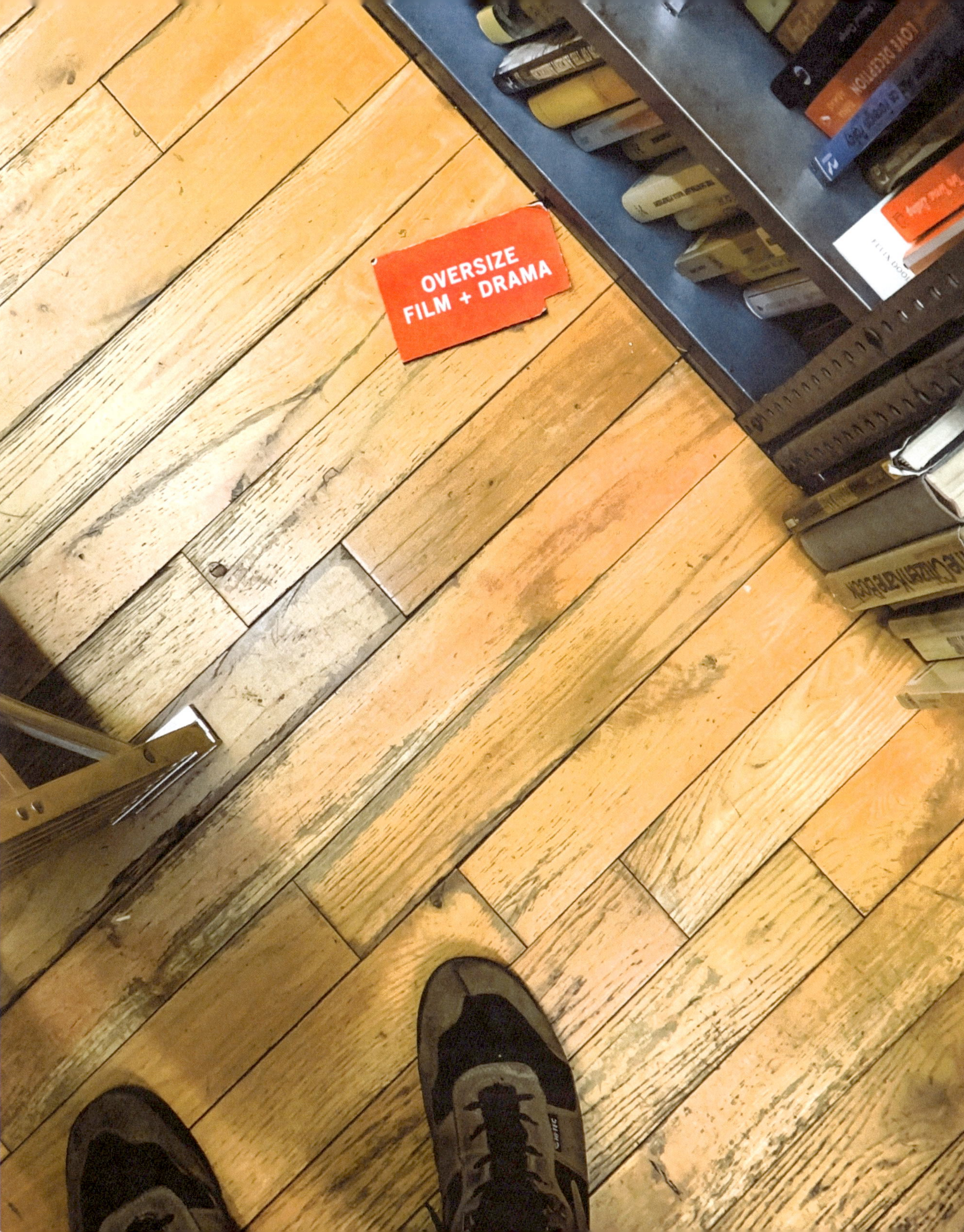
OVERSIZE
FILM + DRAMA

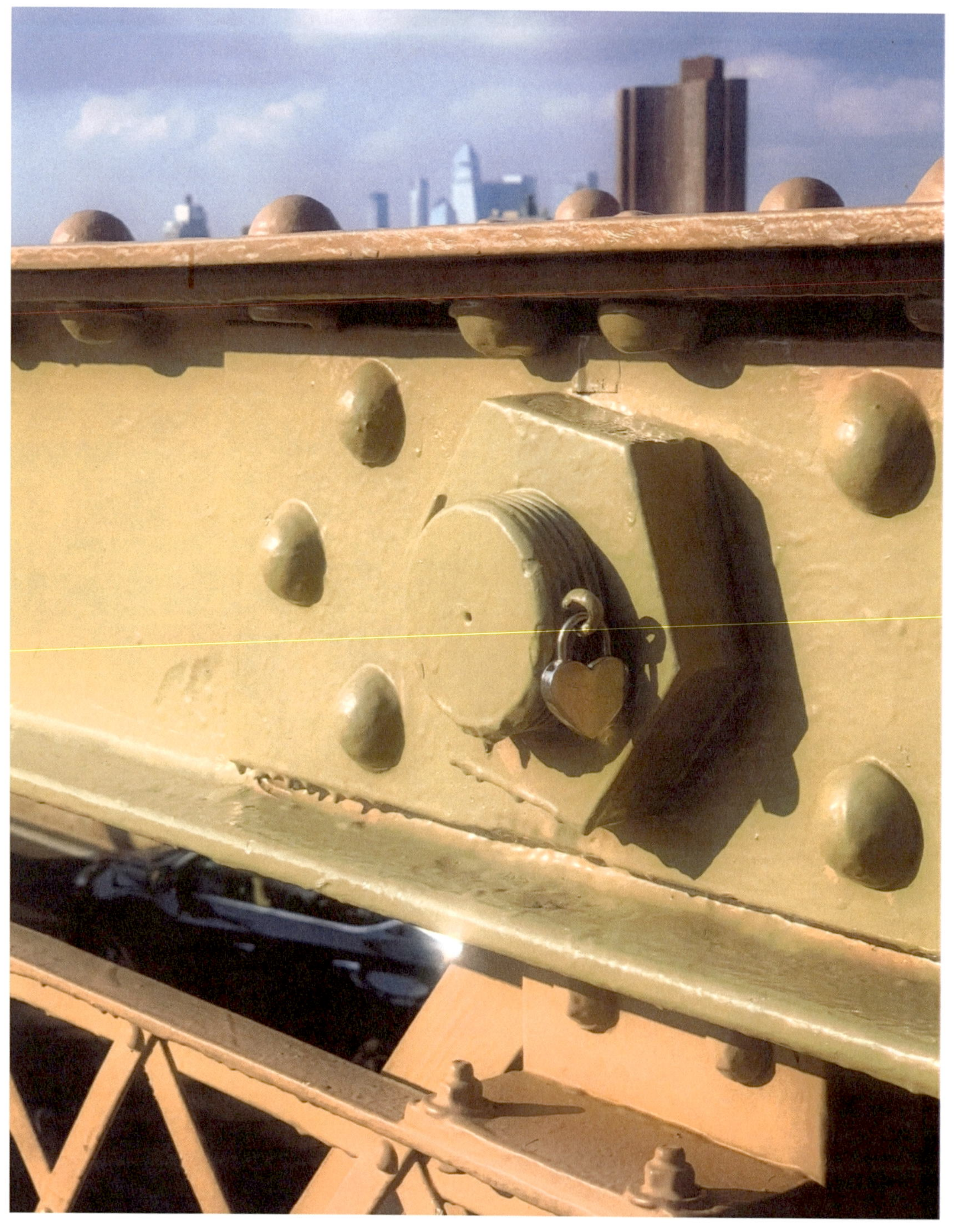

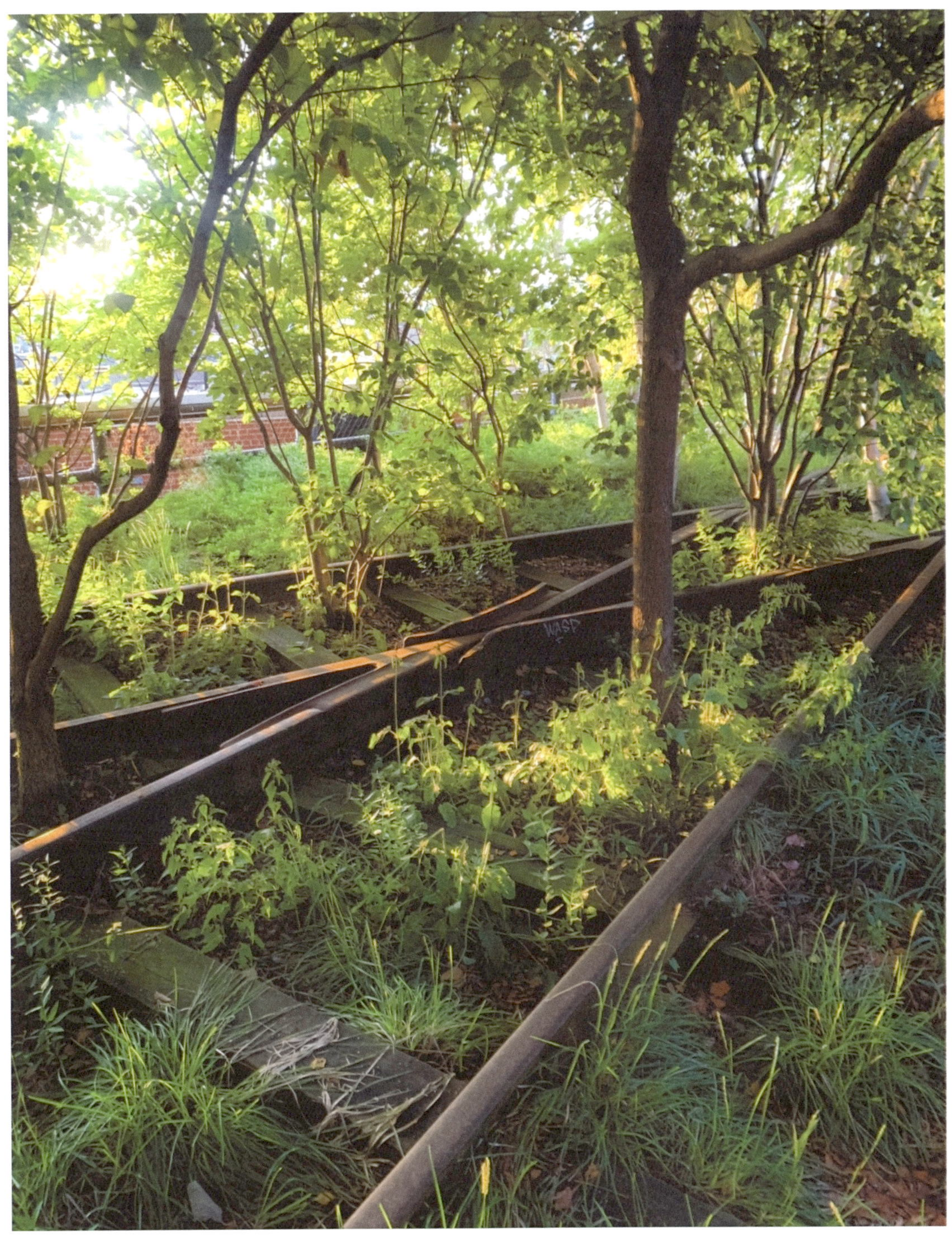

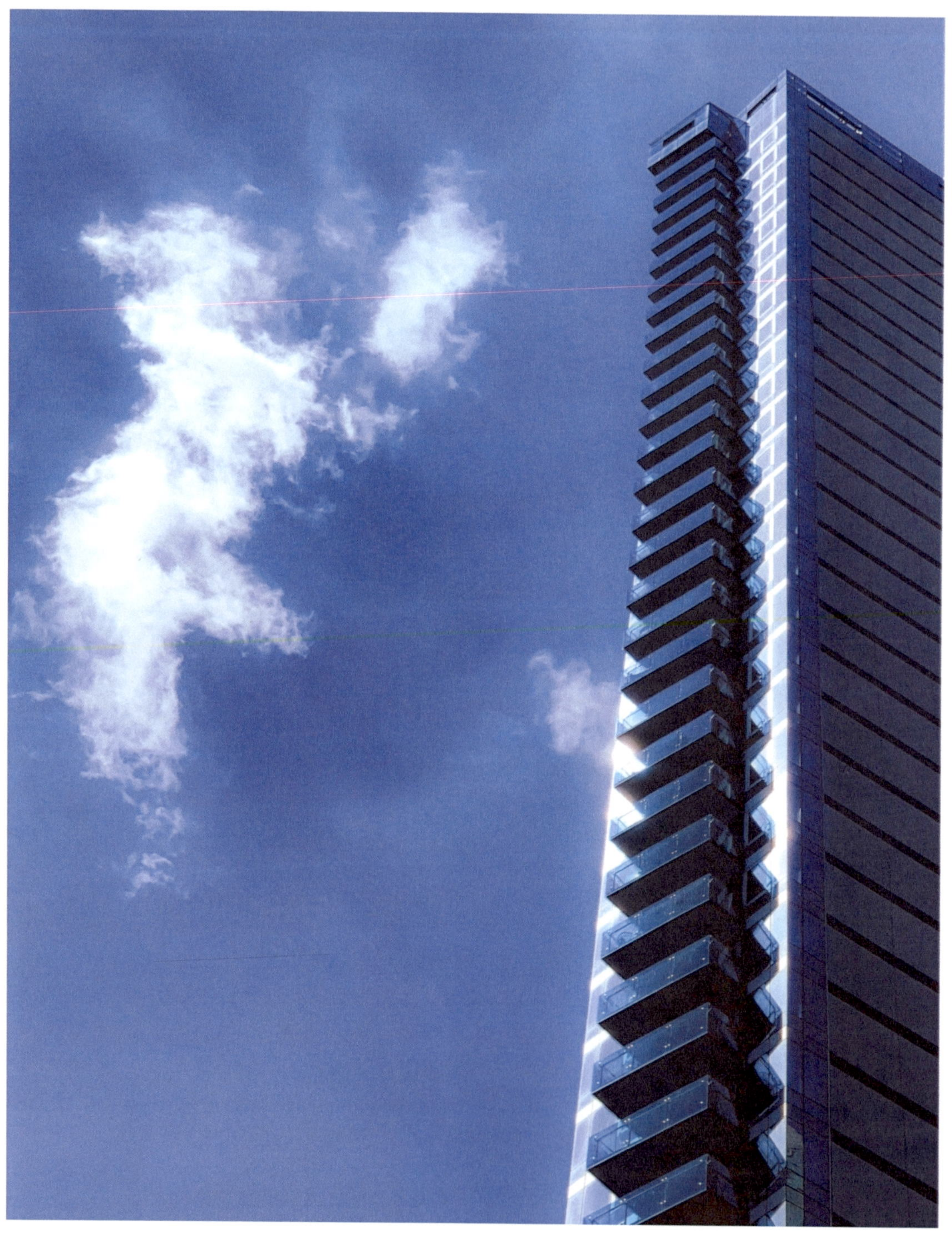

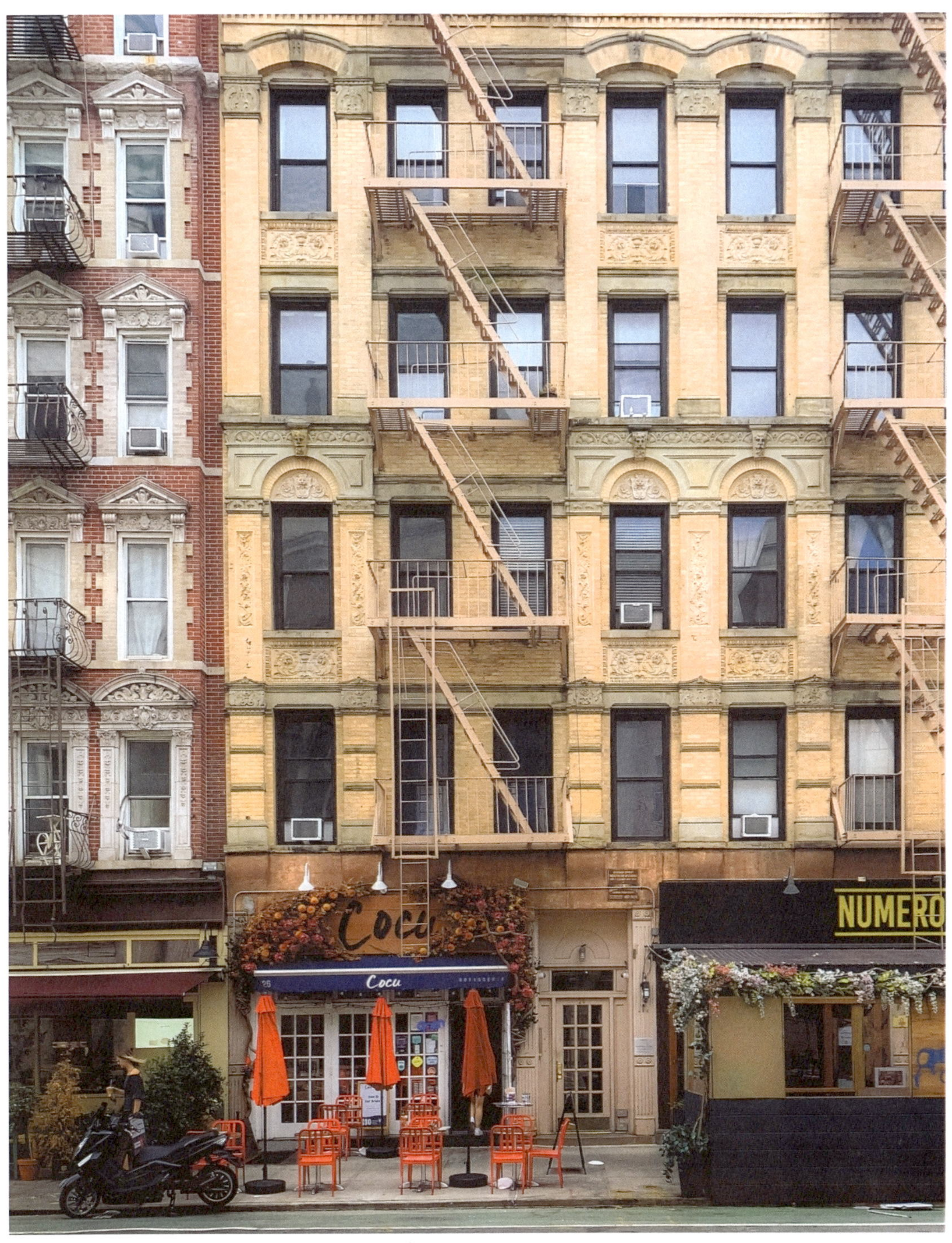

Cocu
Cocu
NUMERO

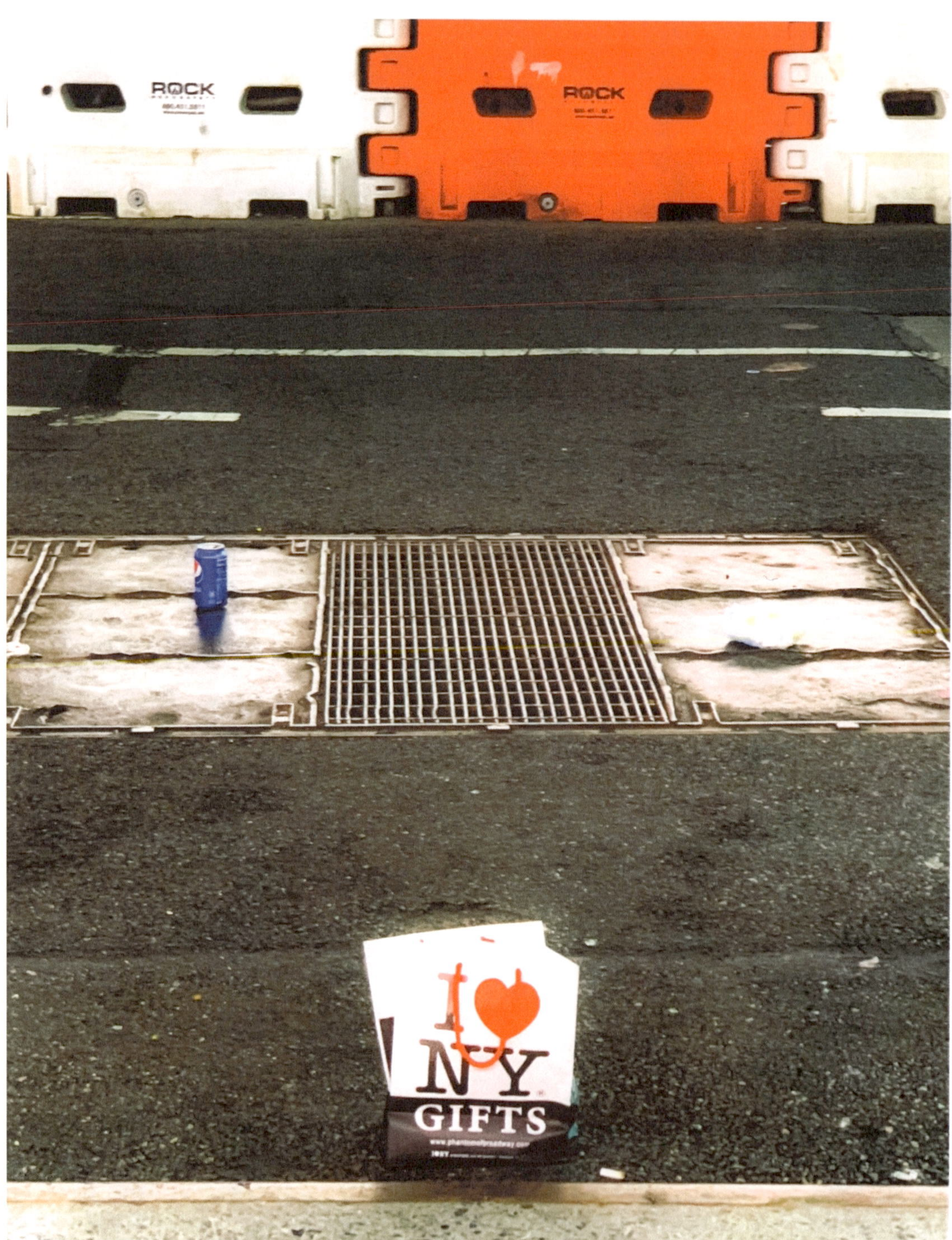
ROCK
ROCK
I ♥ NY
GIFTS

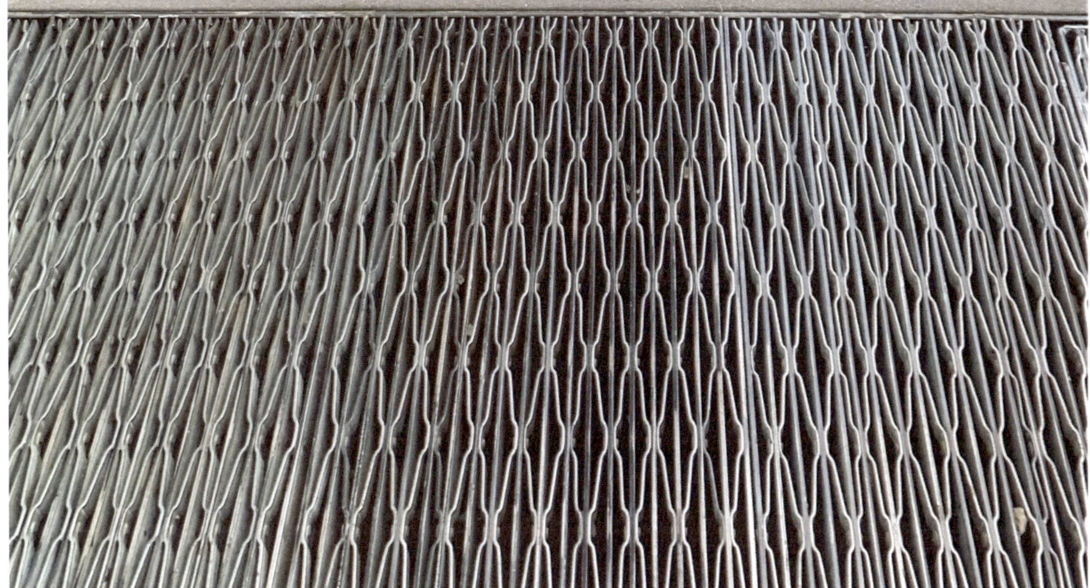

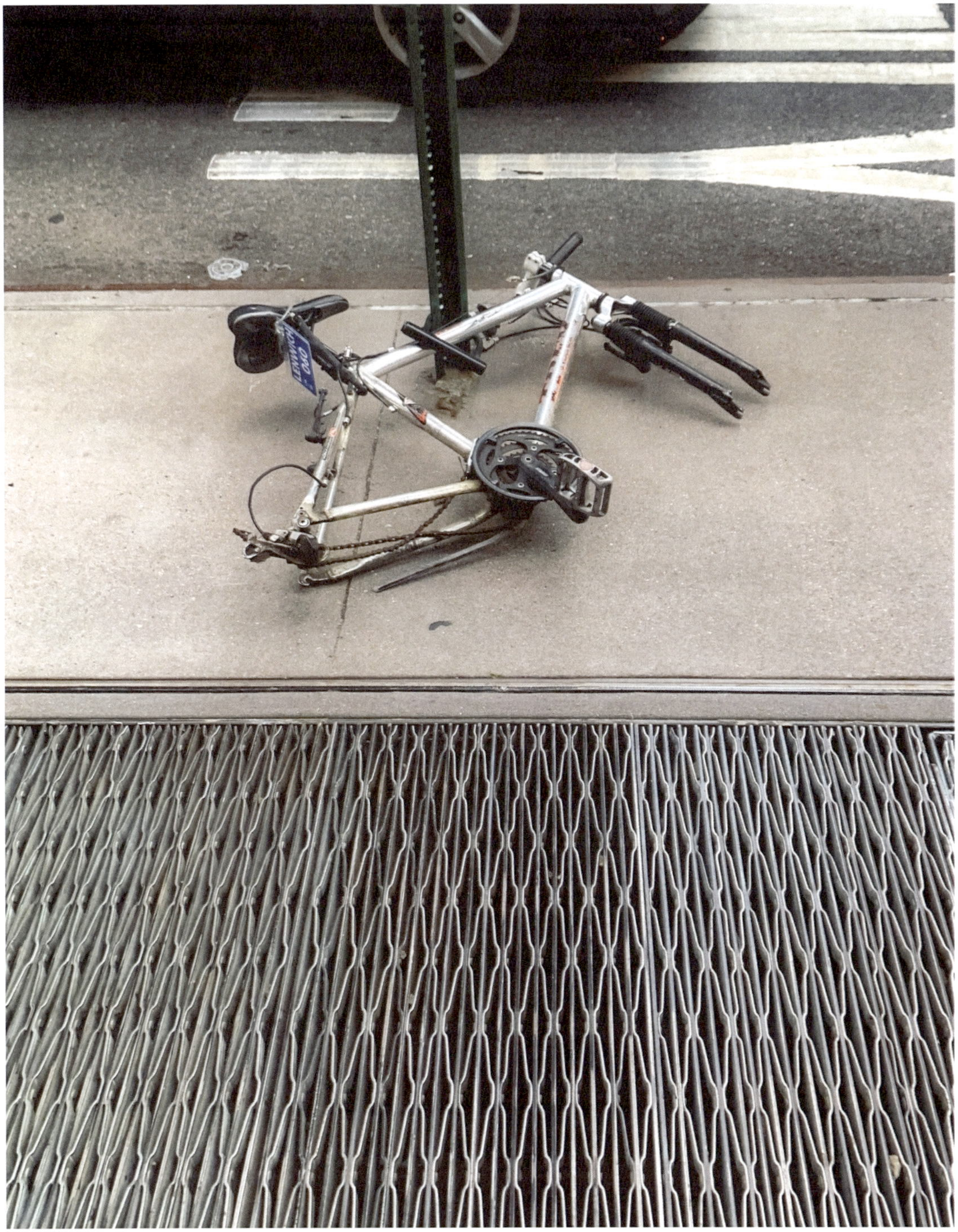

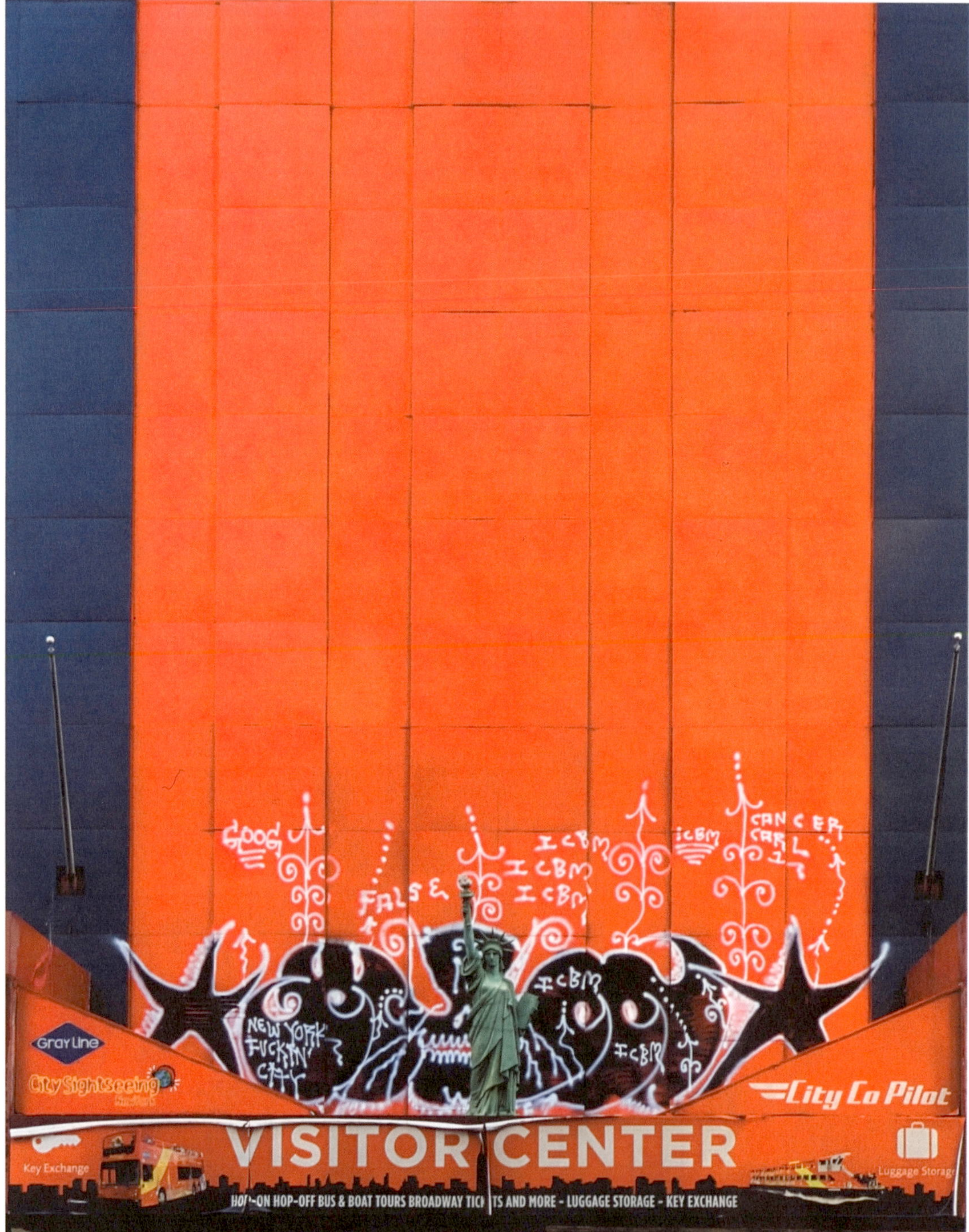

GOOG
FALSE
ICBM
ICBM
ICBM
ICBM
ICBM
CANCER
CARL 1
NEW YORK
FUCKIN'
CITY
Gray Line
City Sightseeing New York
City Co Pilot
Key Exchange
Luggage Storage
VISITOR CENTER
HOP-ON HOP-OFF BUS & BOAT TOURS BROADWAY TICKETS AND MORE - LUGGAGE STORAGE - KEY EXCHANGE

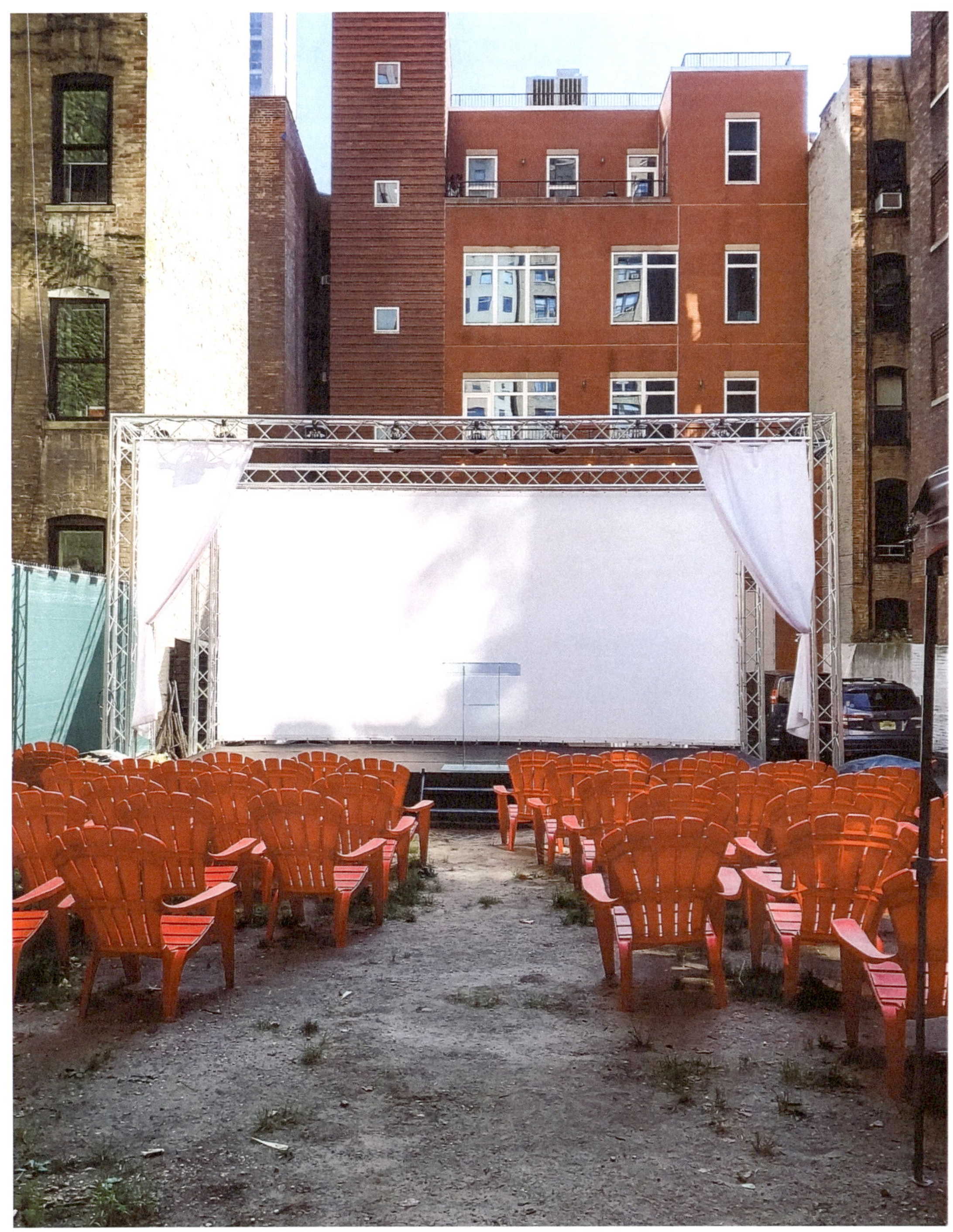

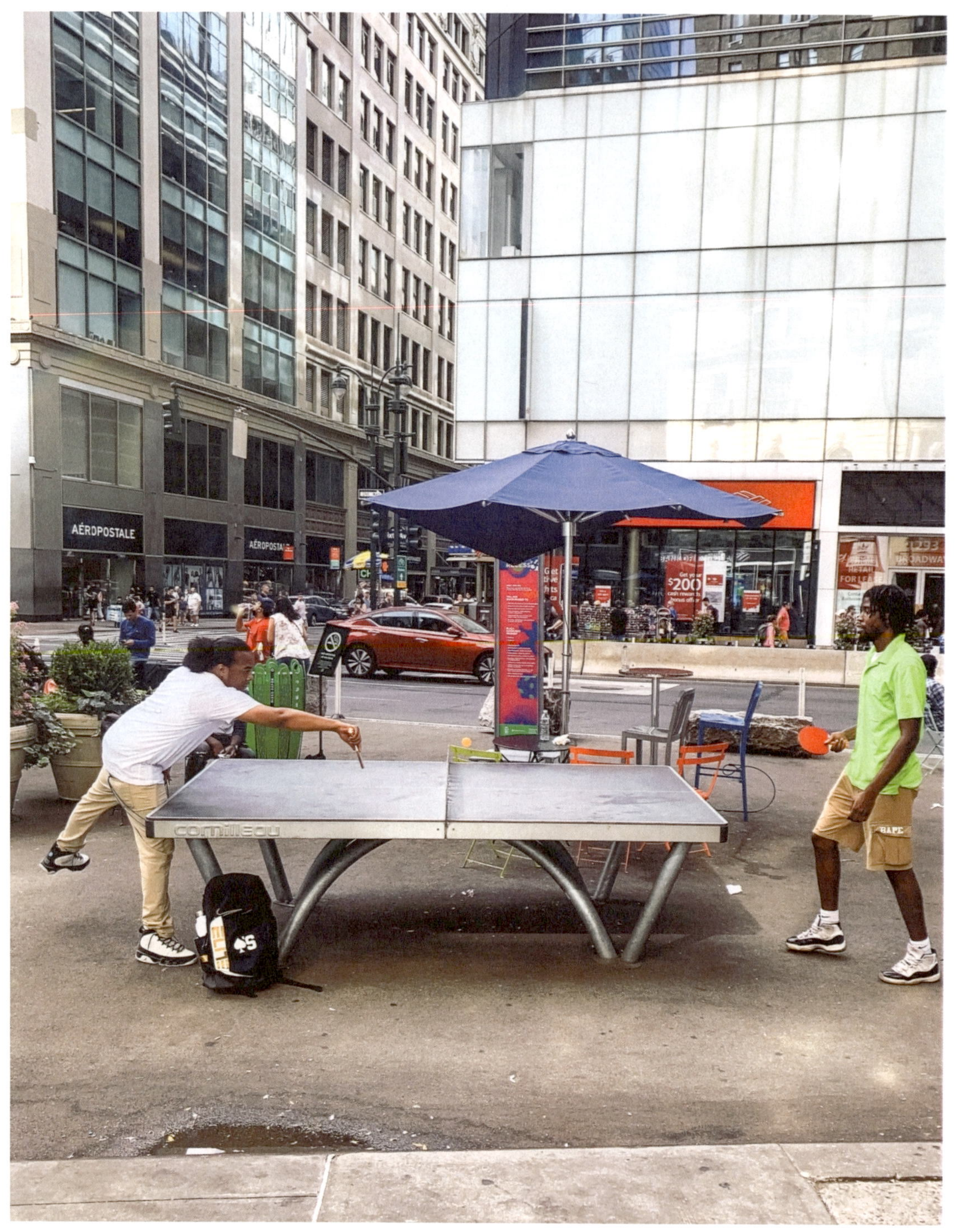
AÉROPOSTALE
AÉROPOSTALE
BAPE

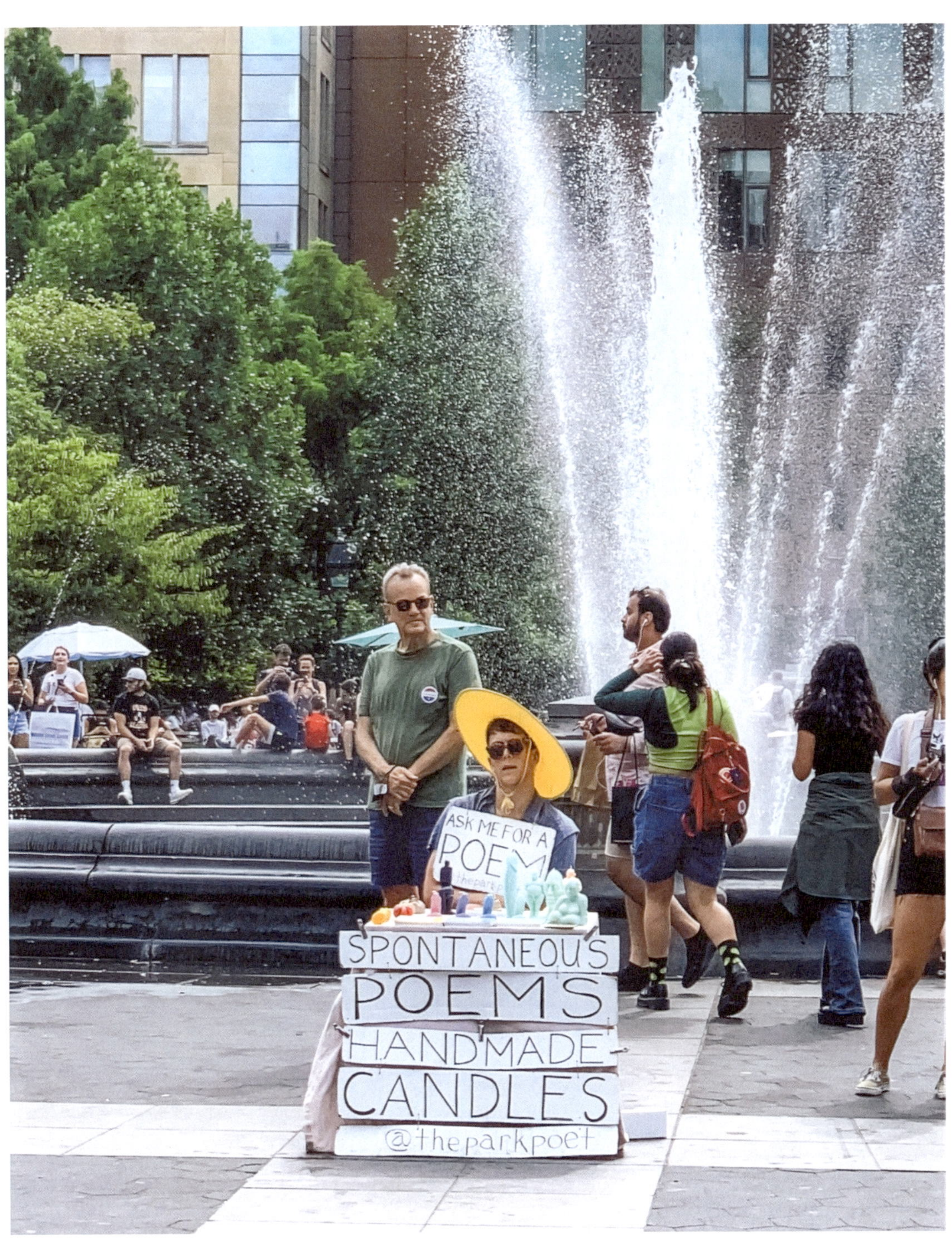

ASK ME FOR A
POEM
theparkp
SPONTANEOUS
POEMS
HANDMADE
CANDLES
@theparkpoet

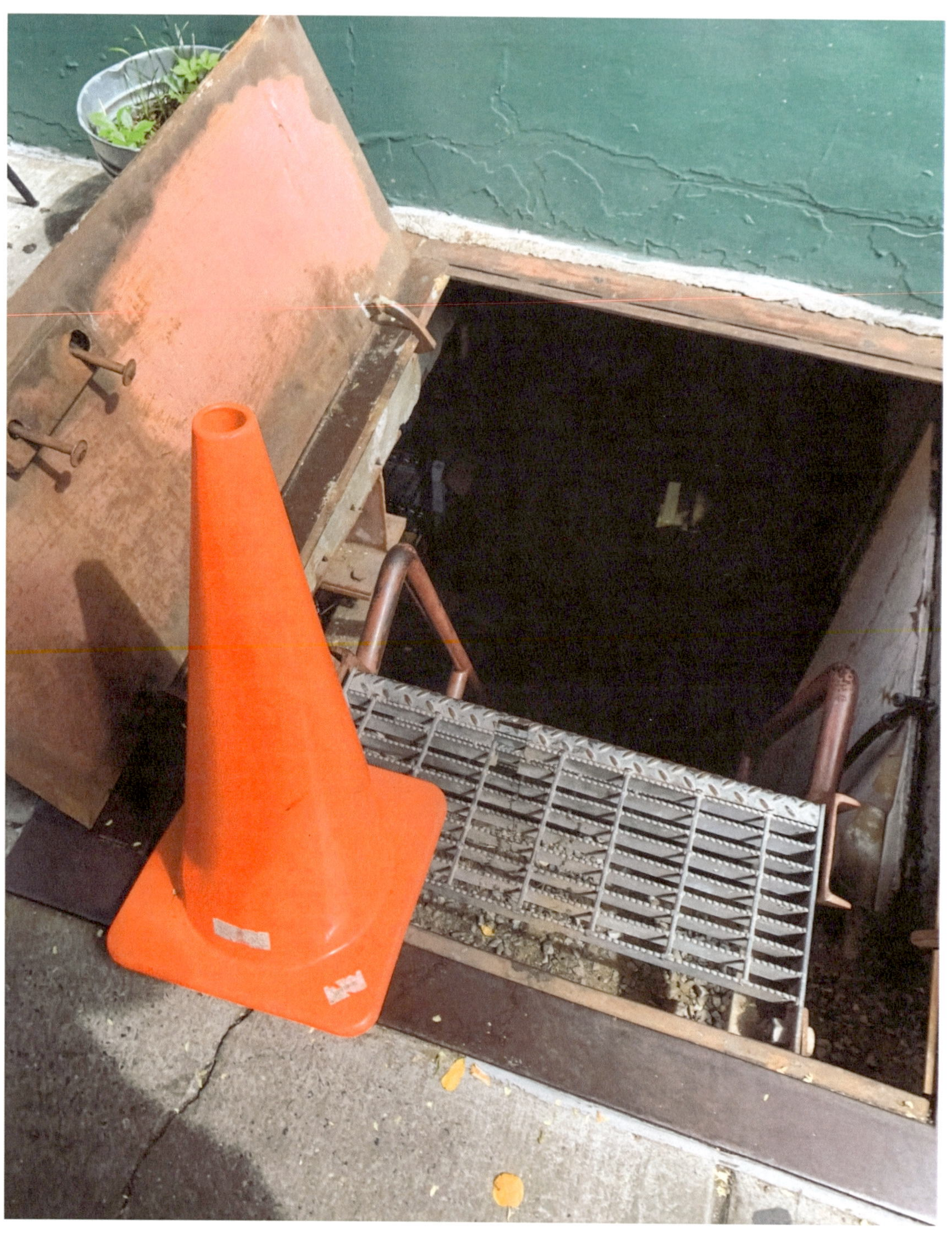

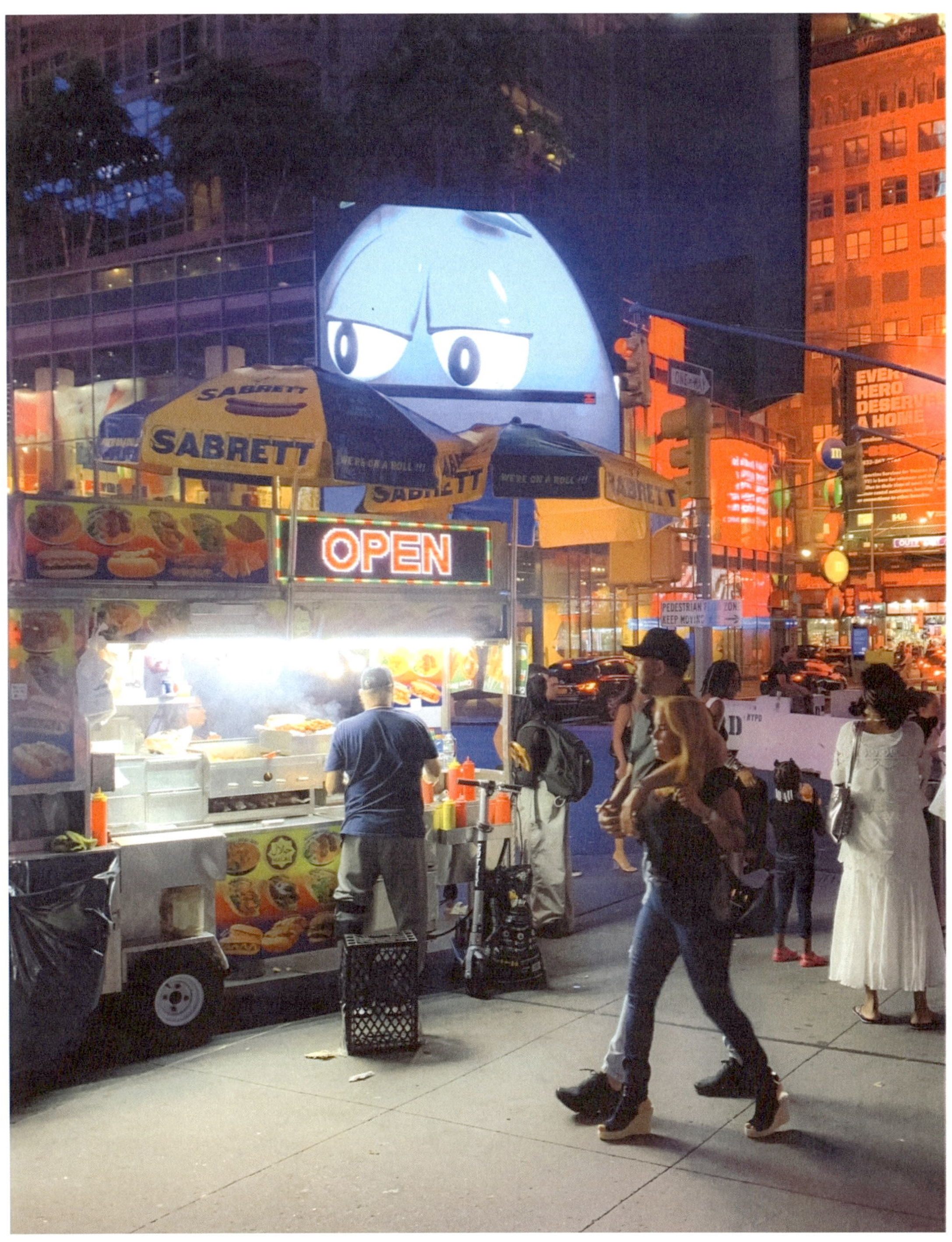
SABRETT
SABRETT
WE'RE ON A ROLL !!!
SABRETT
WE'RE ON A ROLL !!!
SABRETT
OPEN
EVERY
HERO
DESERVES
A HOME
PEDESTRIAN
KEEP MOVING

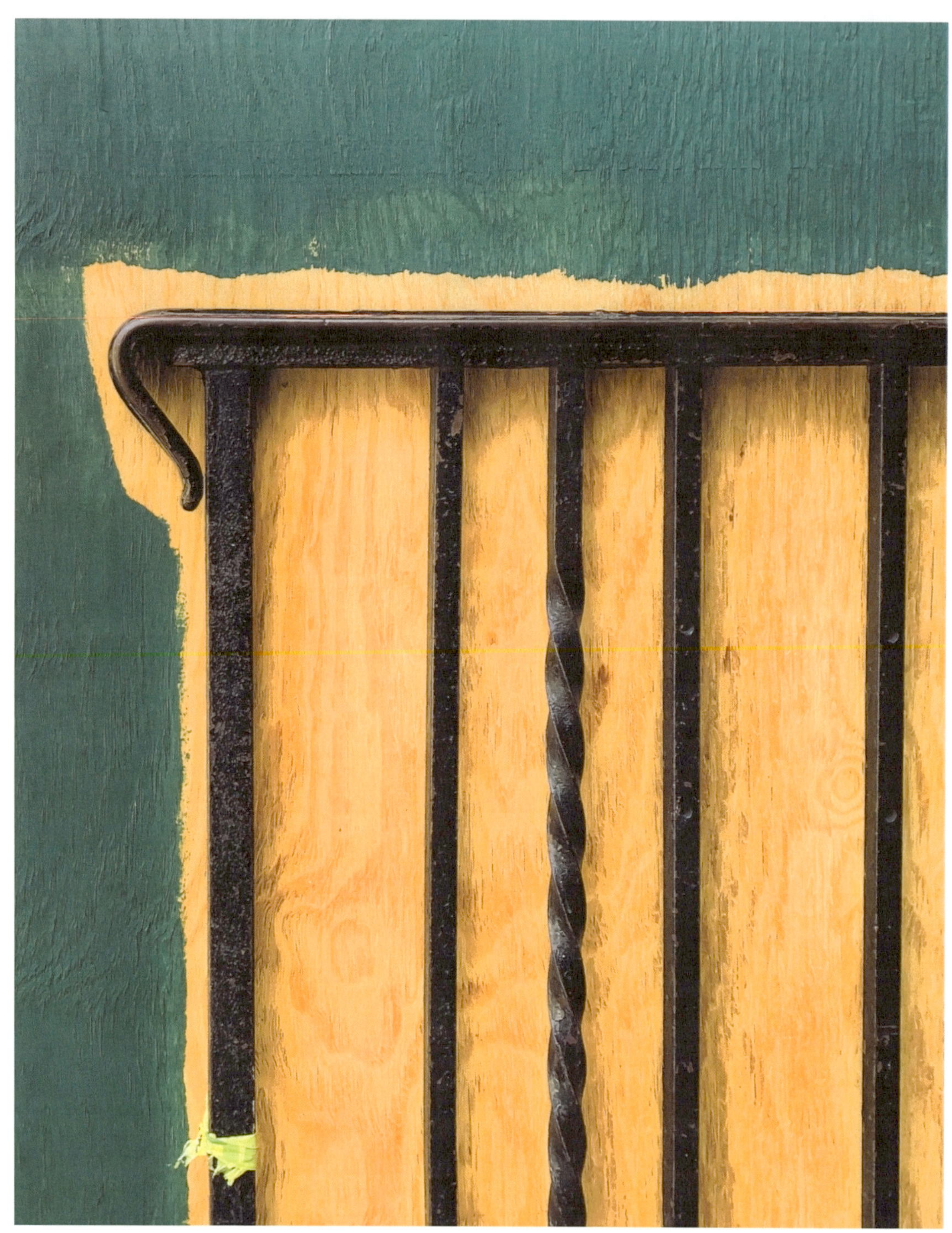

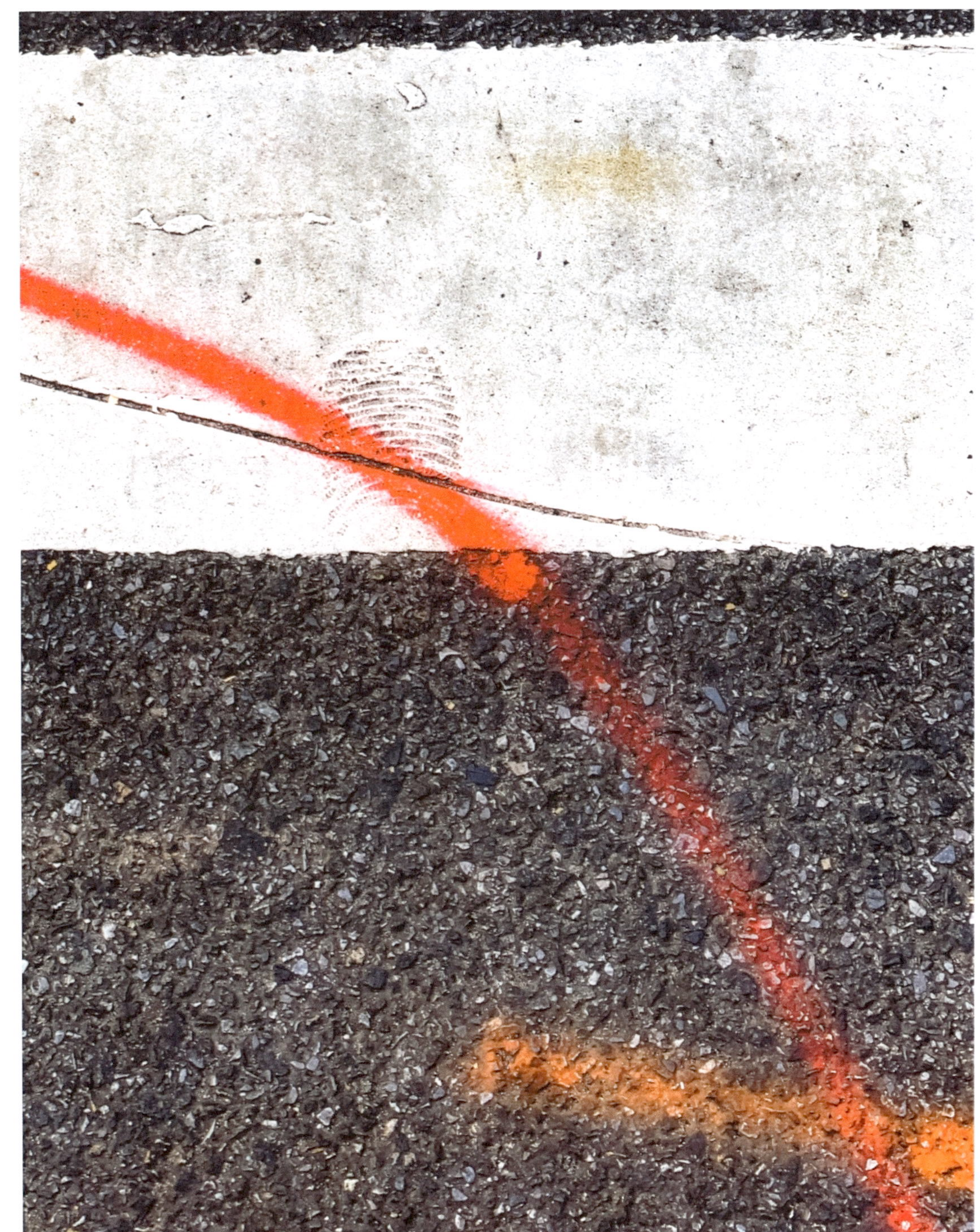

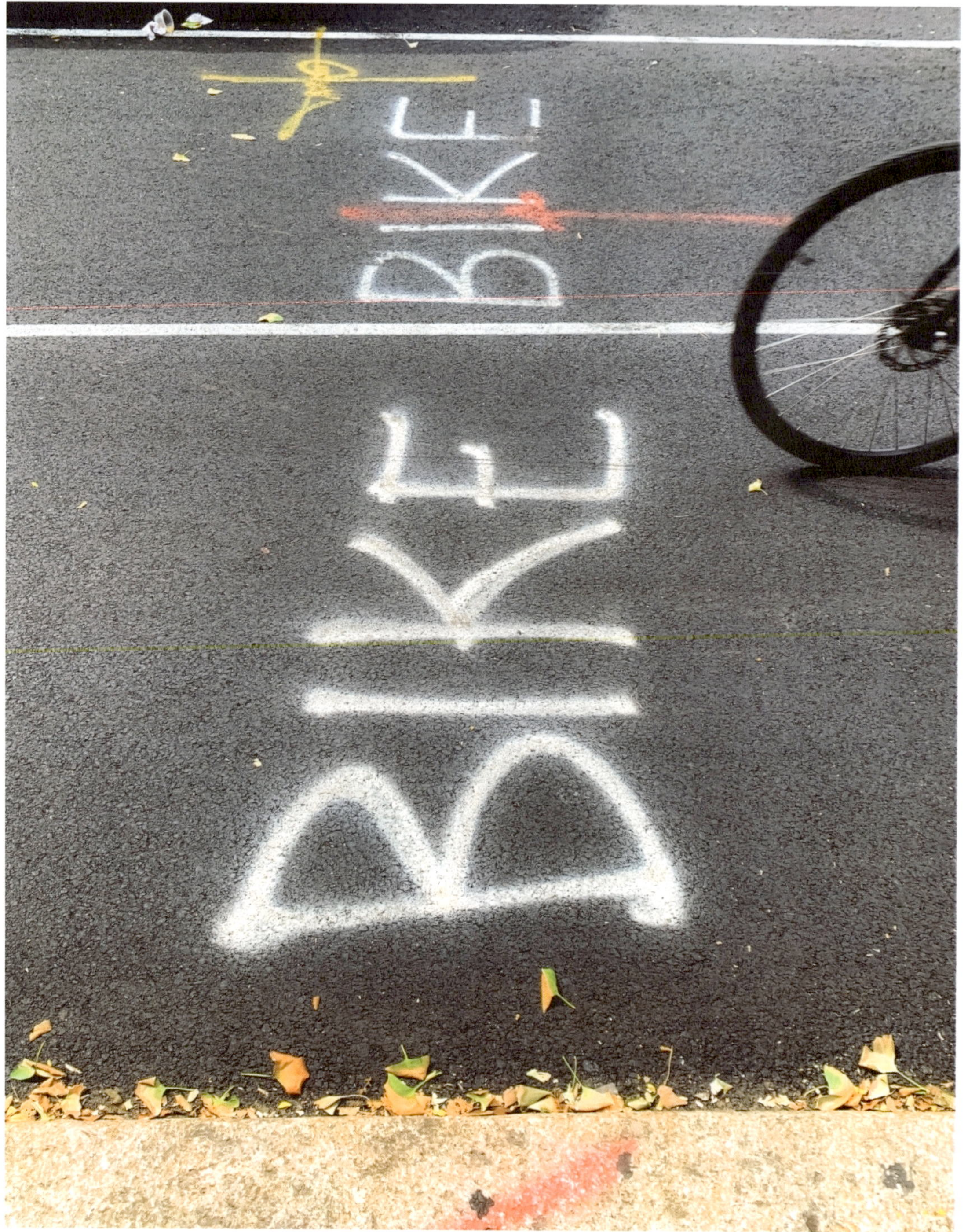

BIKE
BIKE
BIKE

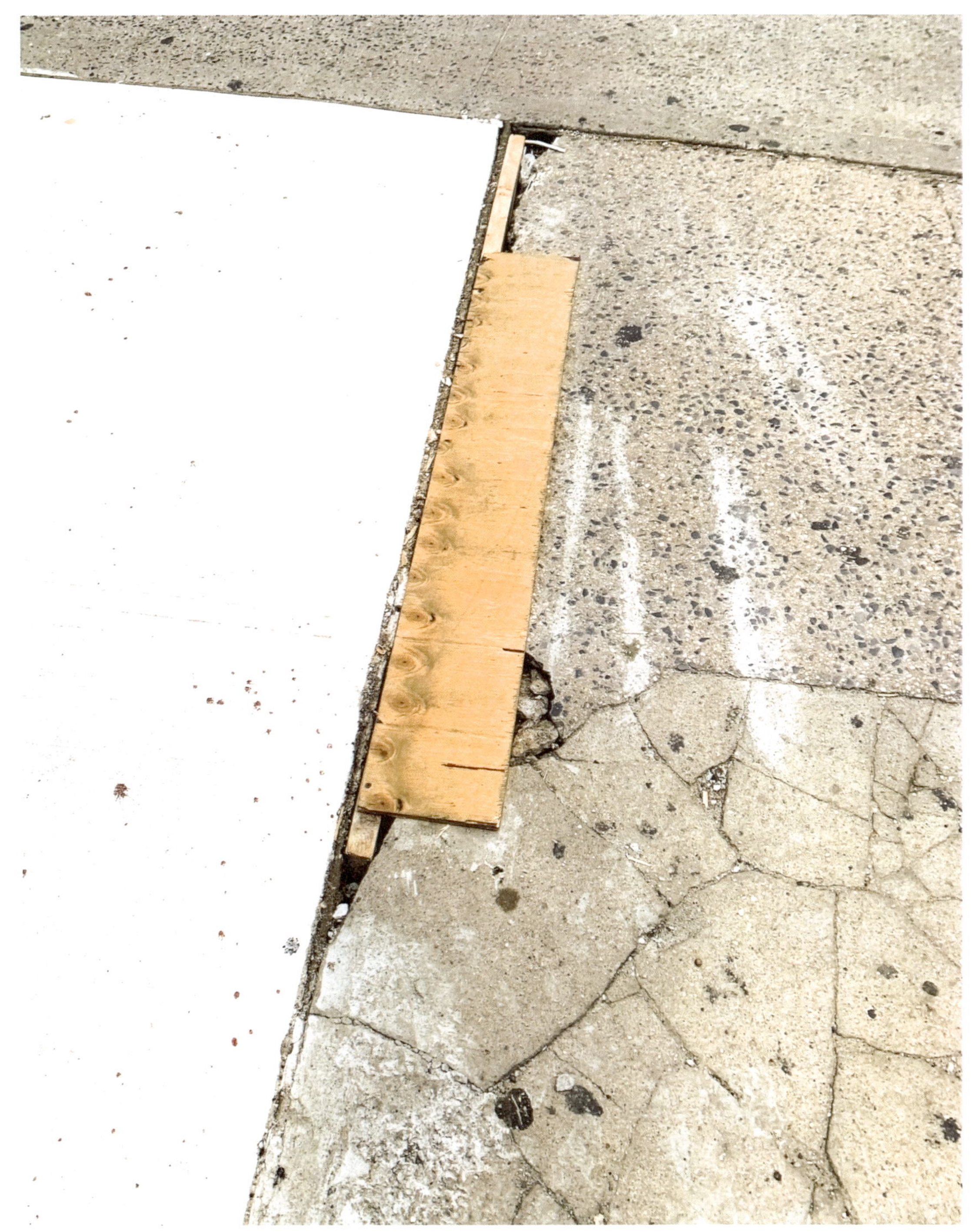

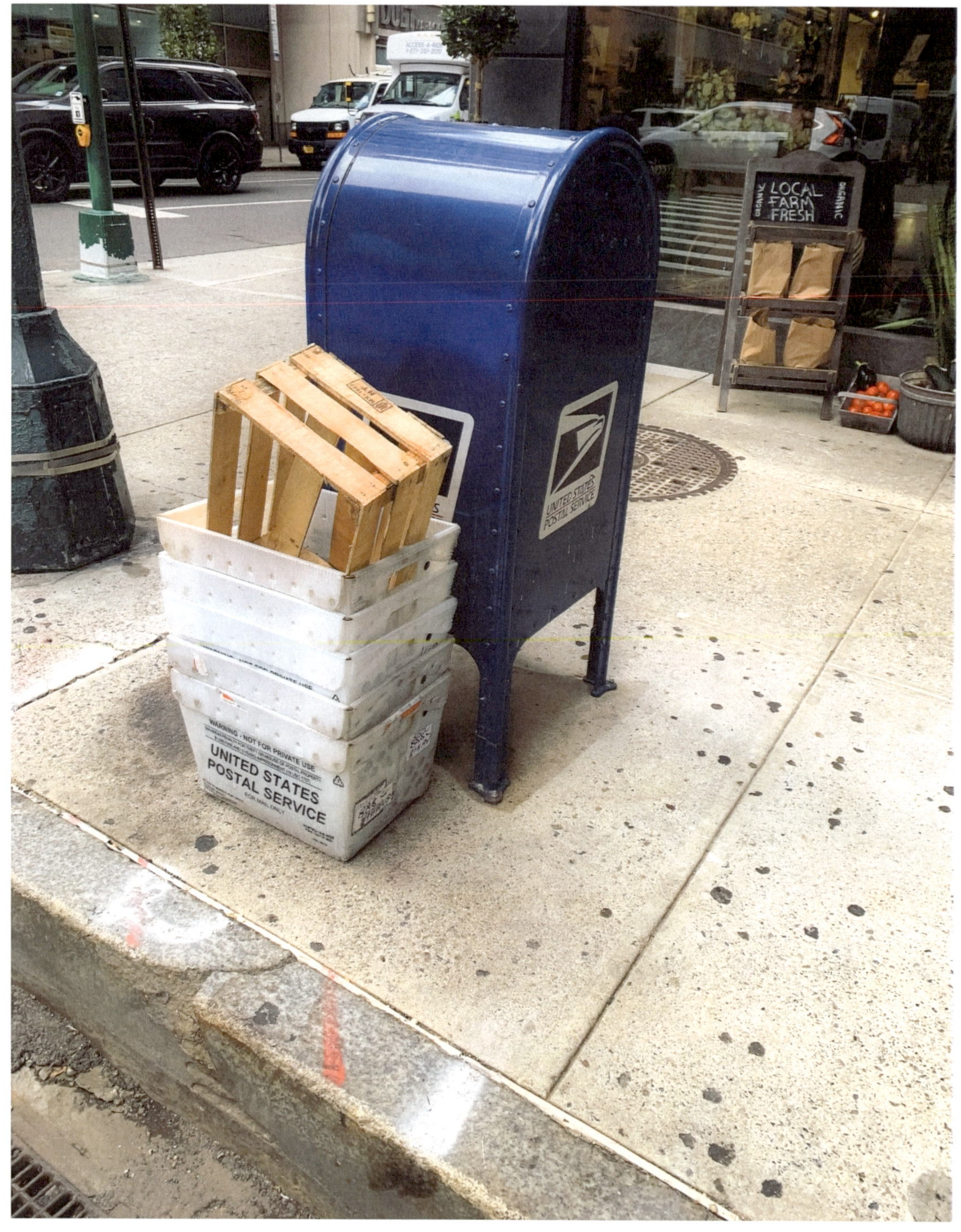

LOCAL
FARM
FRESH
ORGANIC
ORGANIC
UNITED STATES
POSTAL SERVICE
WARNING · NOT FOR PRIVATE USE
UNITED STATES
POSTAL SERVICE
FOR MAIL ONLY

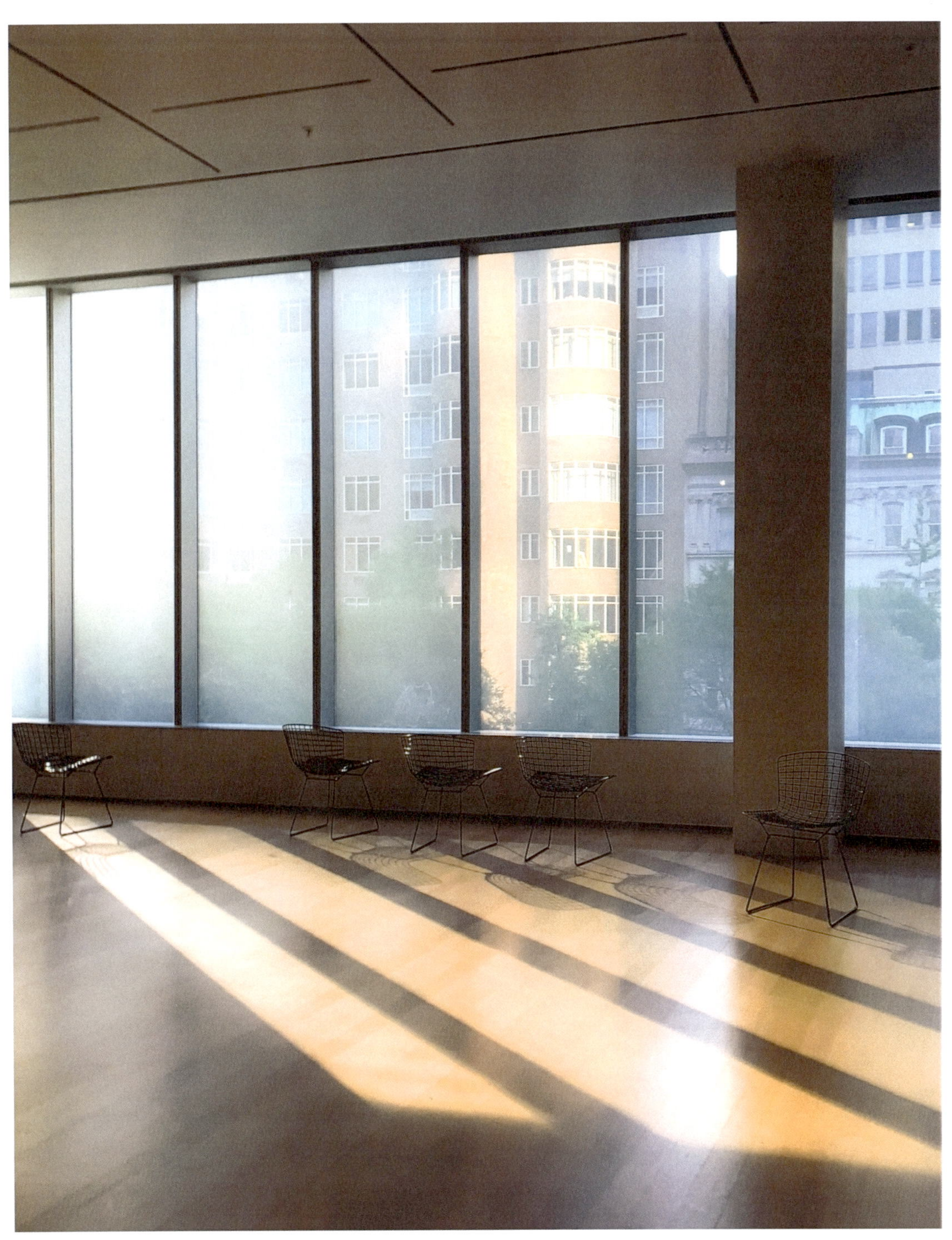

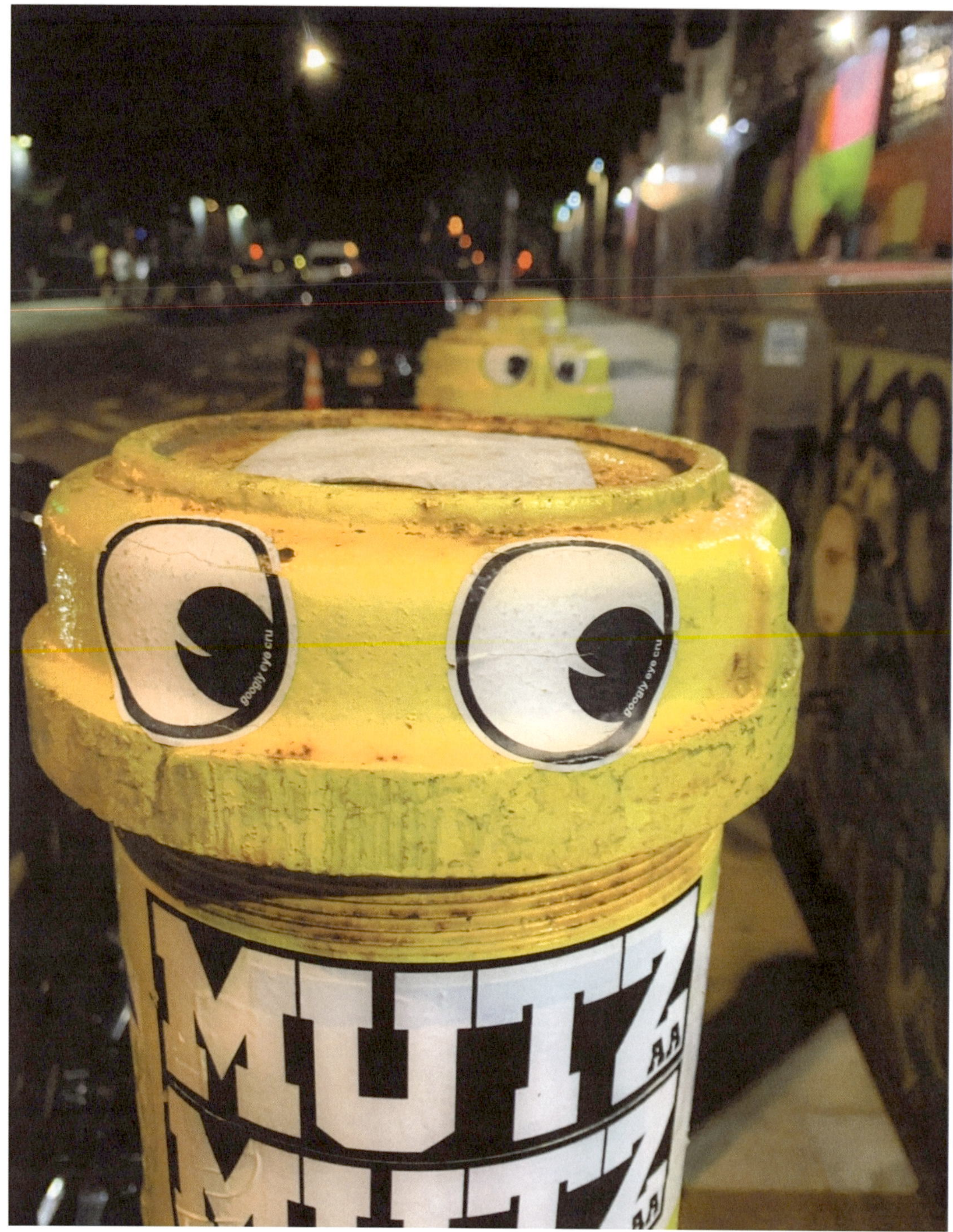

googly eye cru
googly eye cru
MUTZ
MUTZ

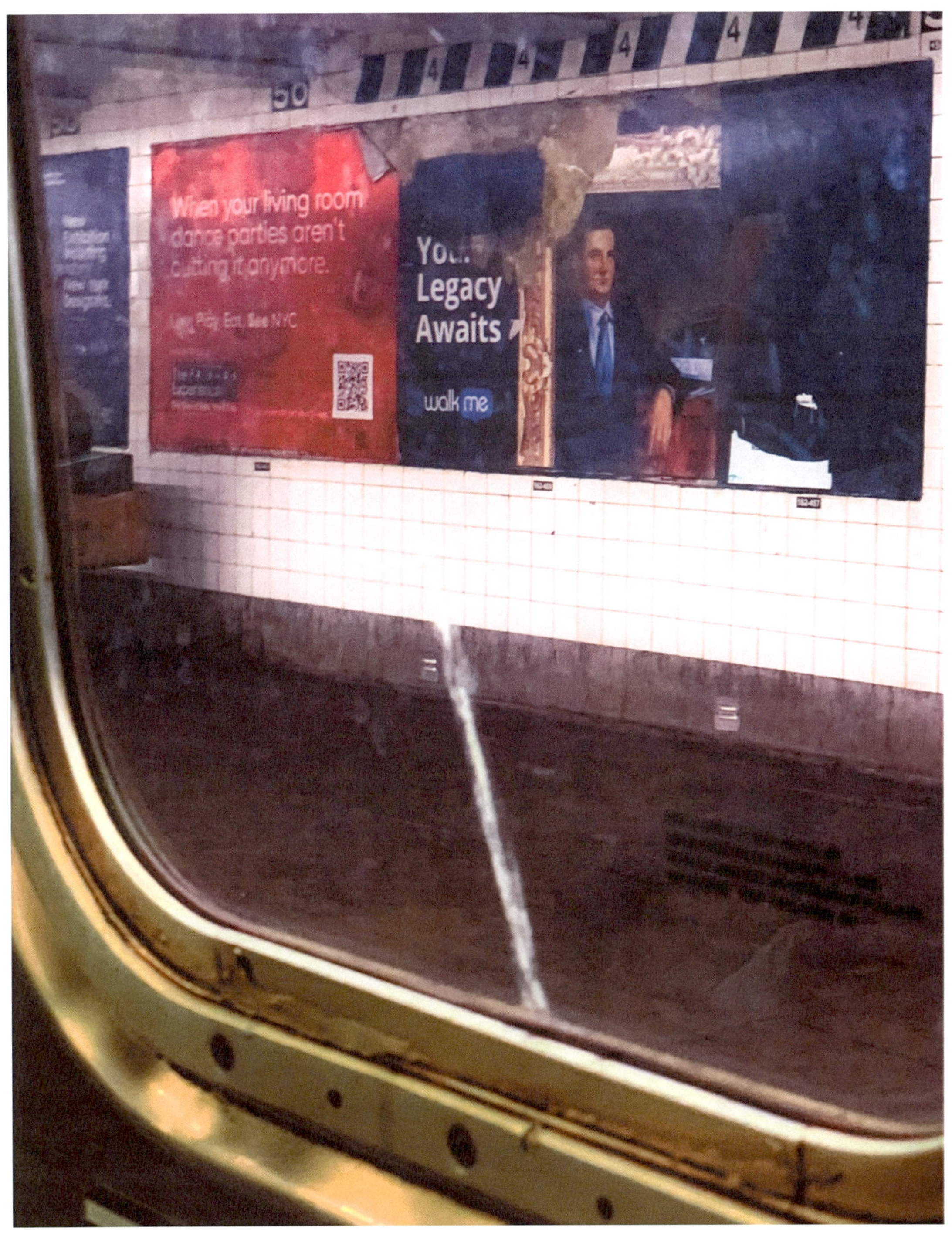
50
When your living room
dance parties aren't
cutting it anymore.
Play. Eat. See NYC
Your
Legacy
Awaits
walk me

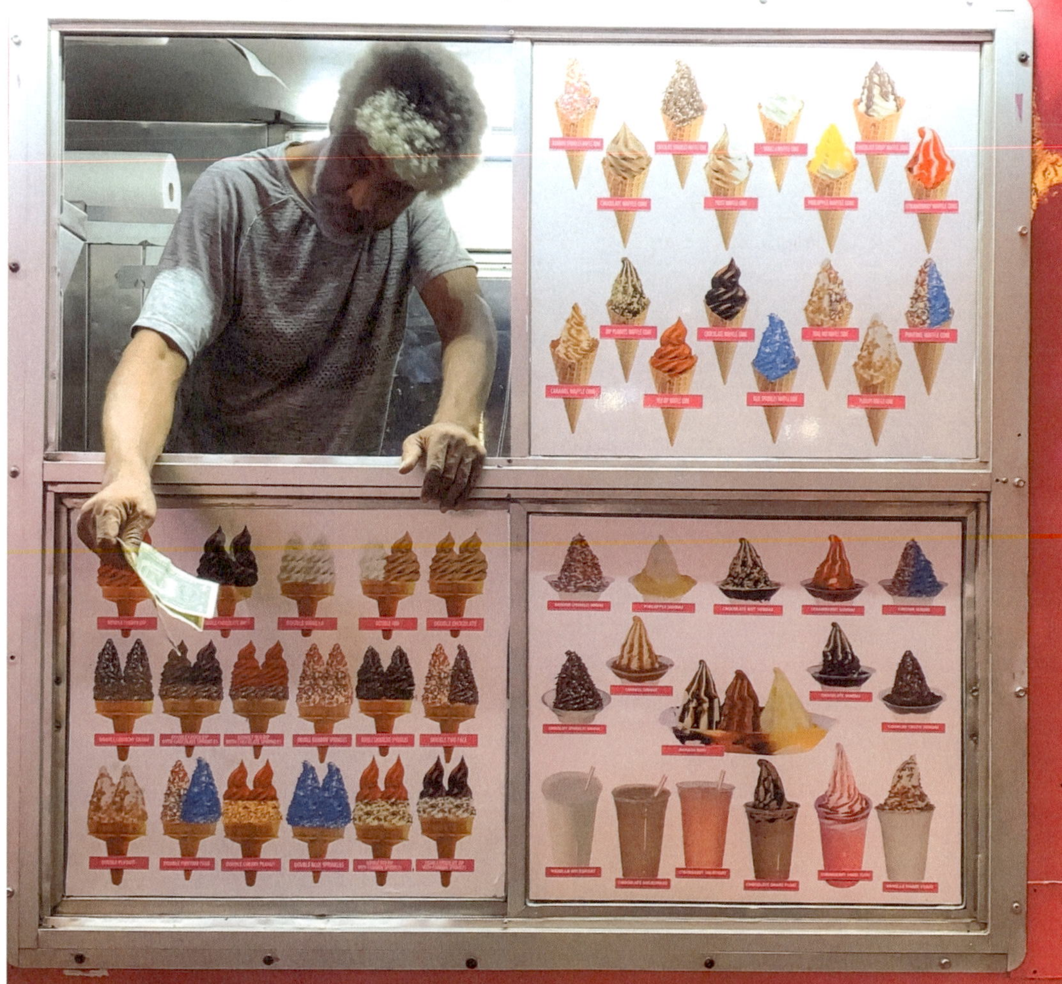

ES SHAKES CONES

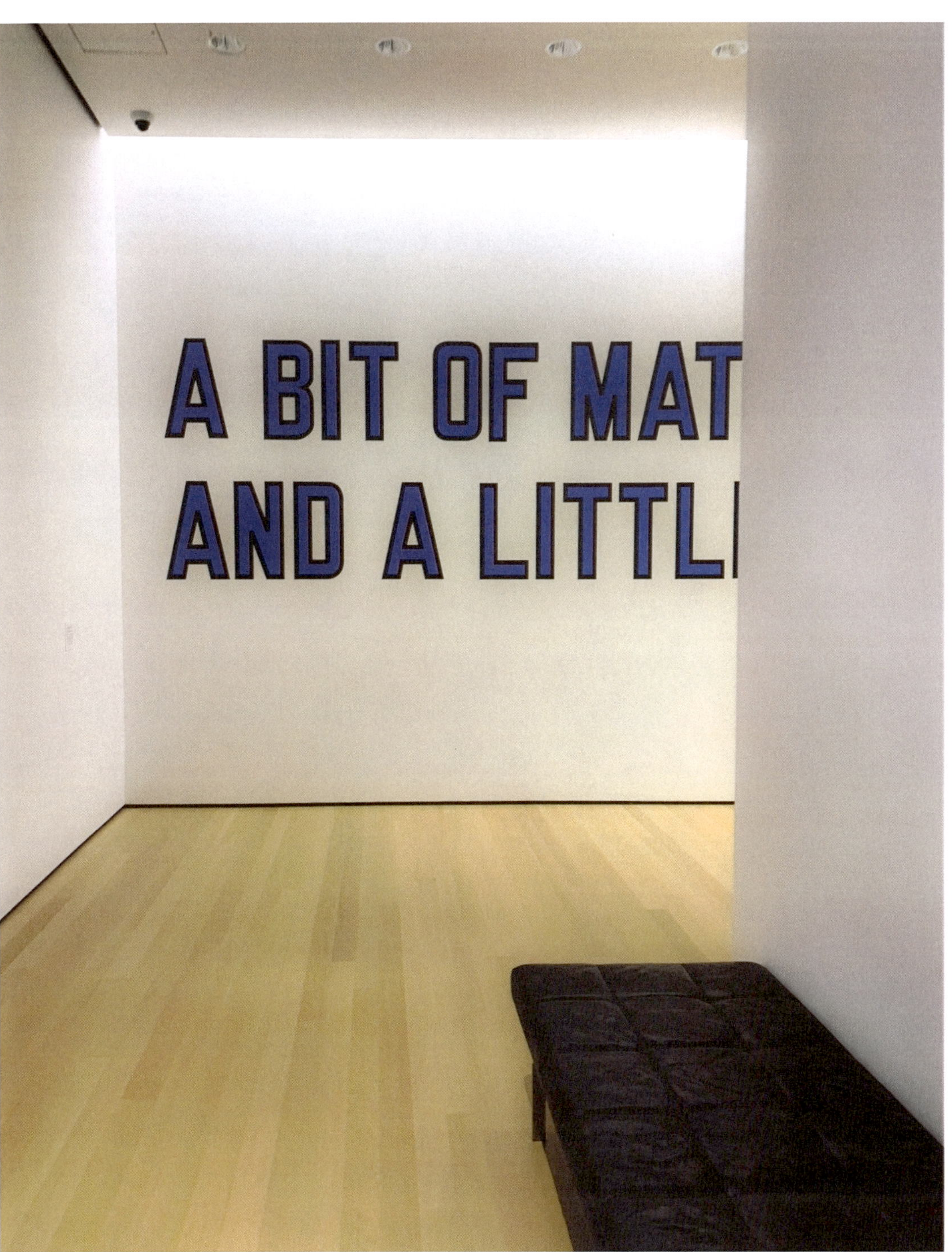
A BIT OF MAT
AND A LITTL

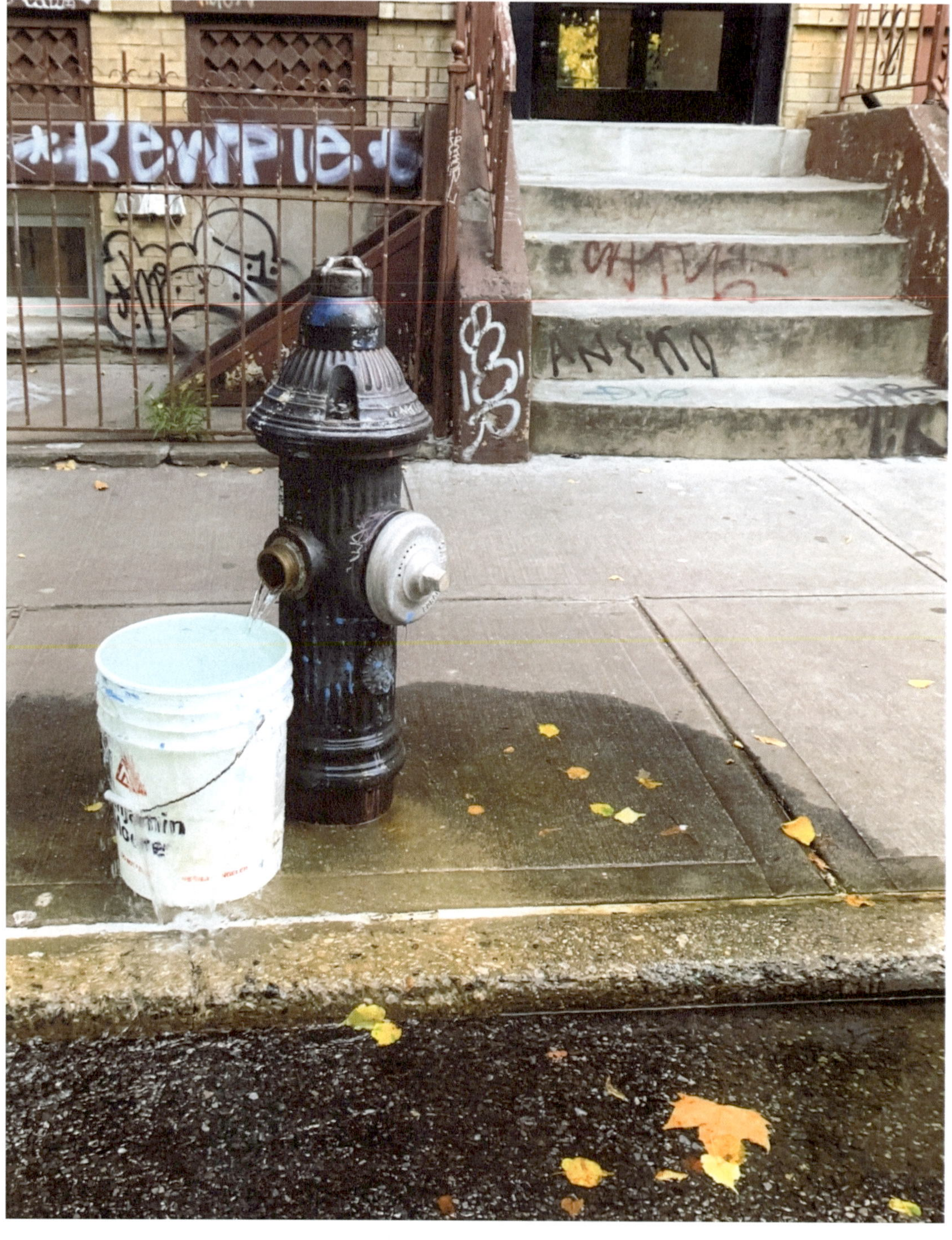

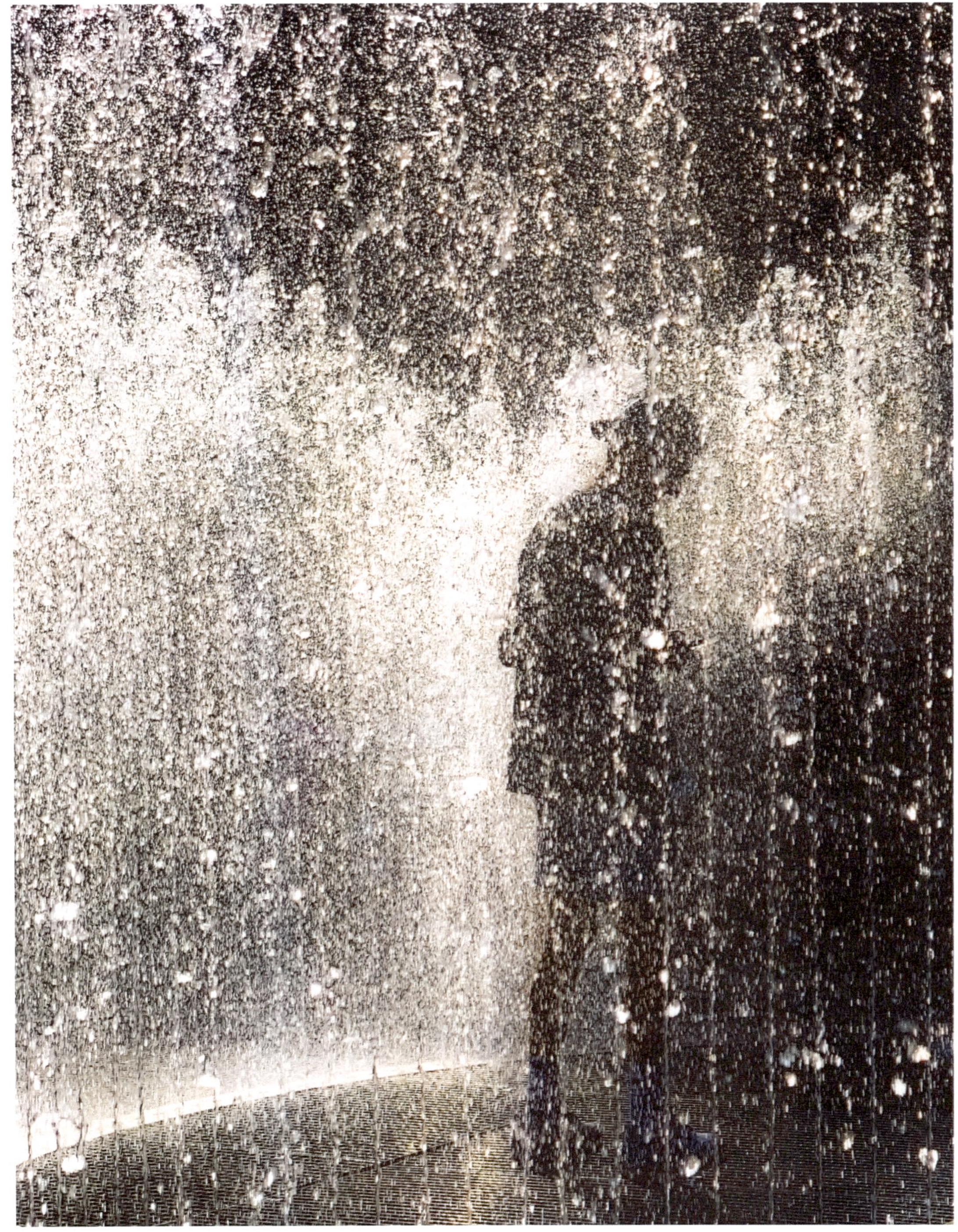

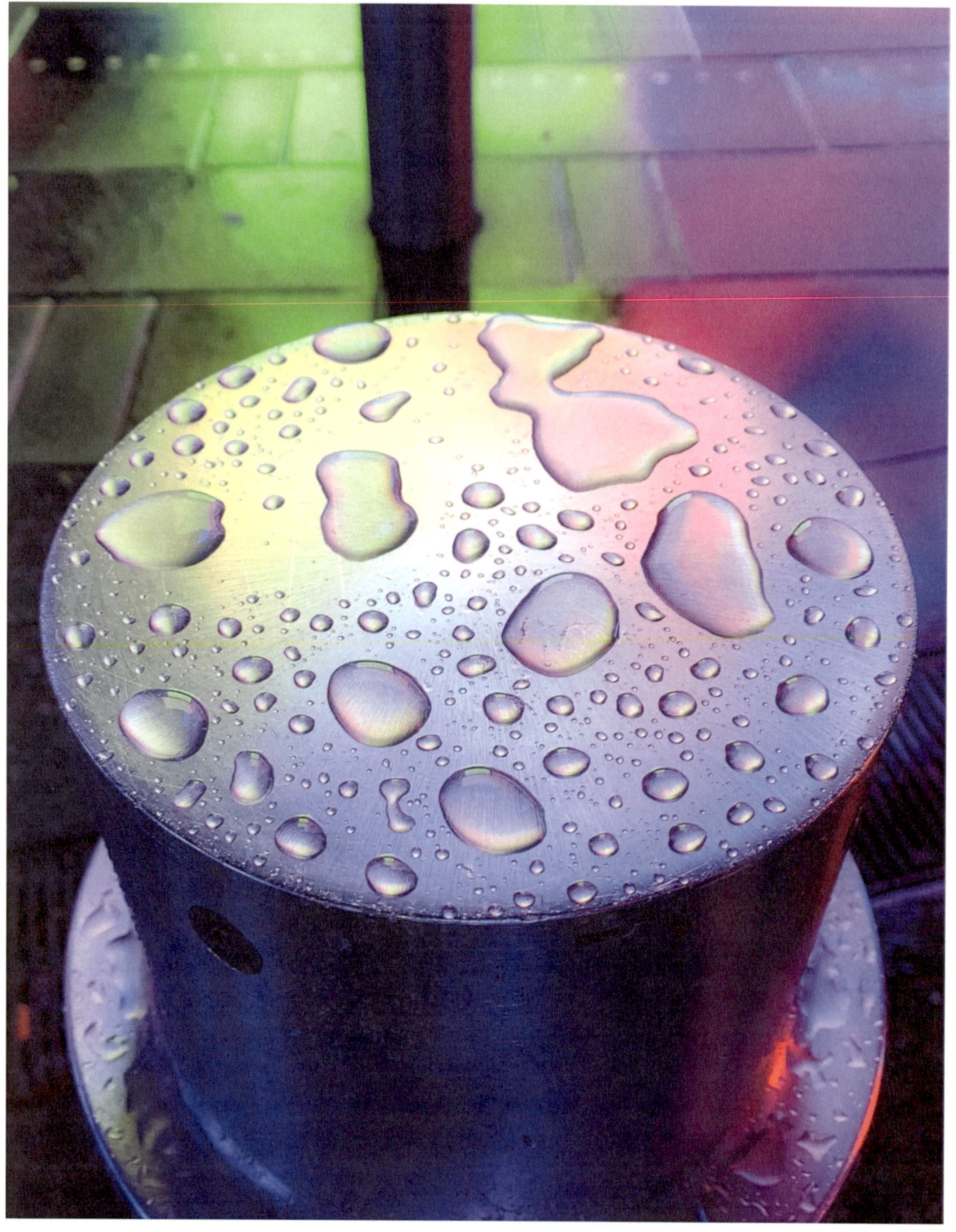

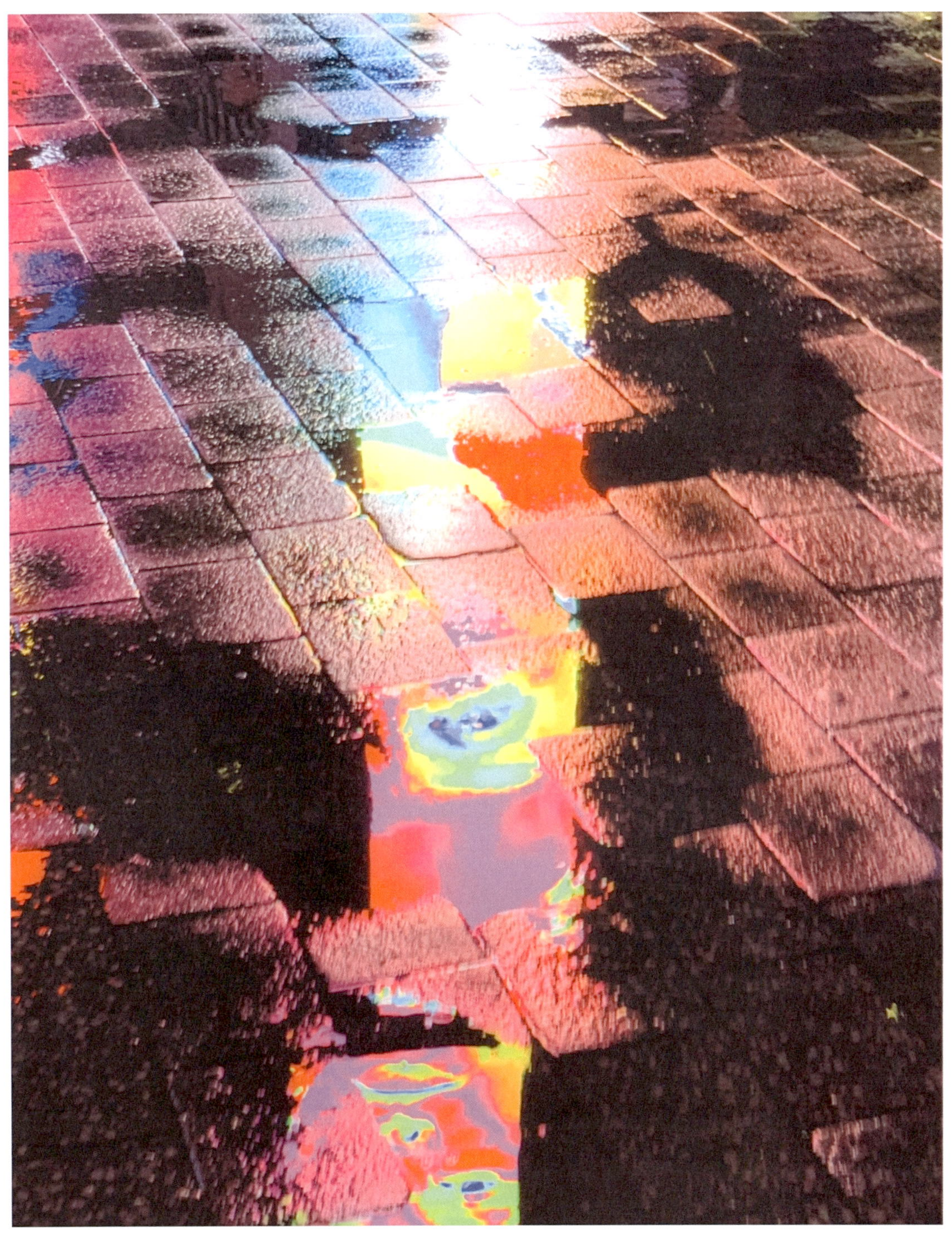

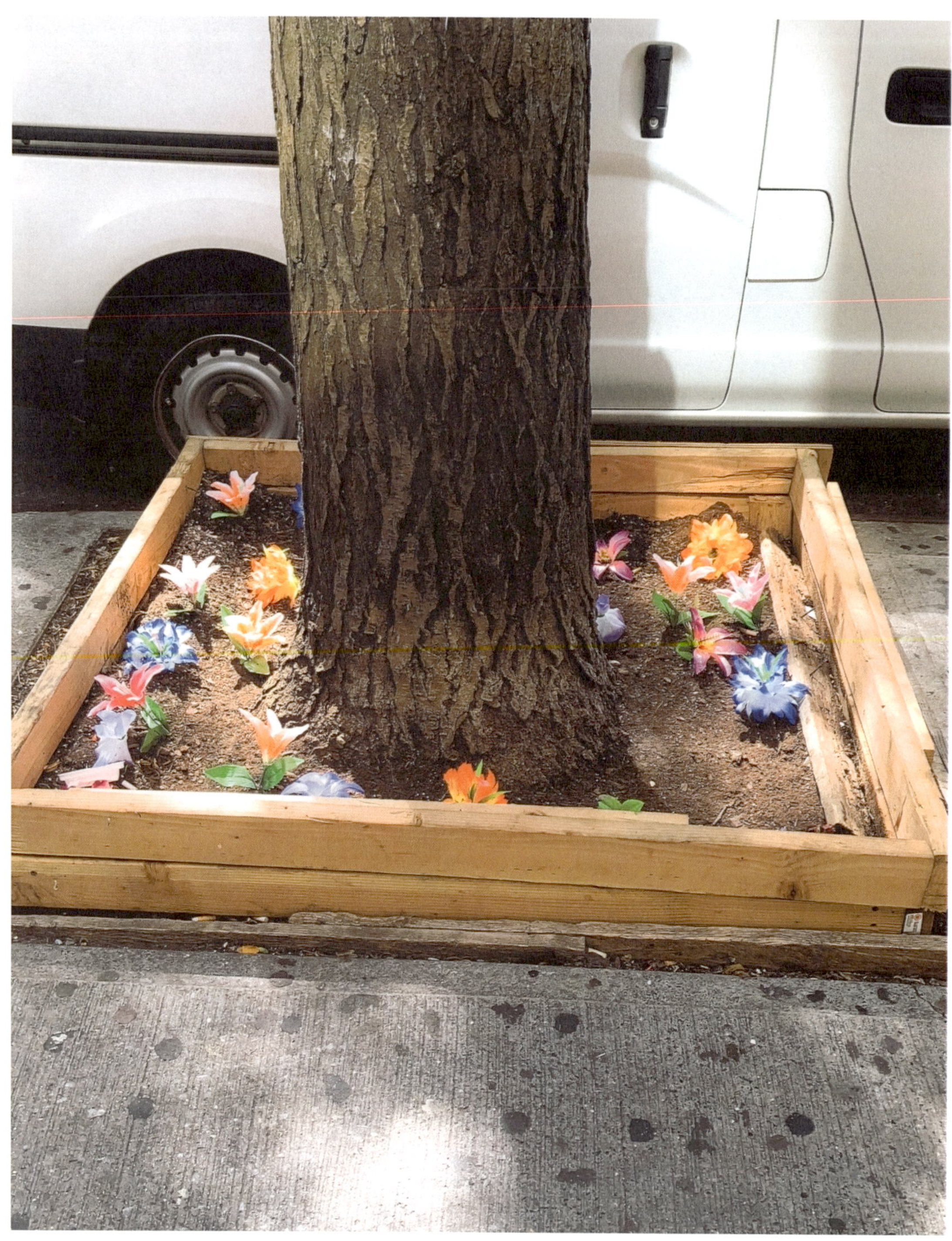

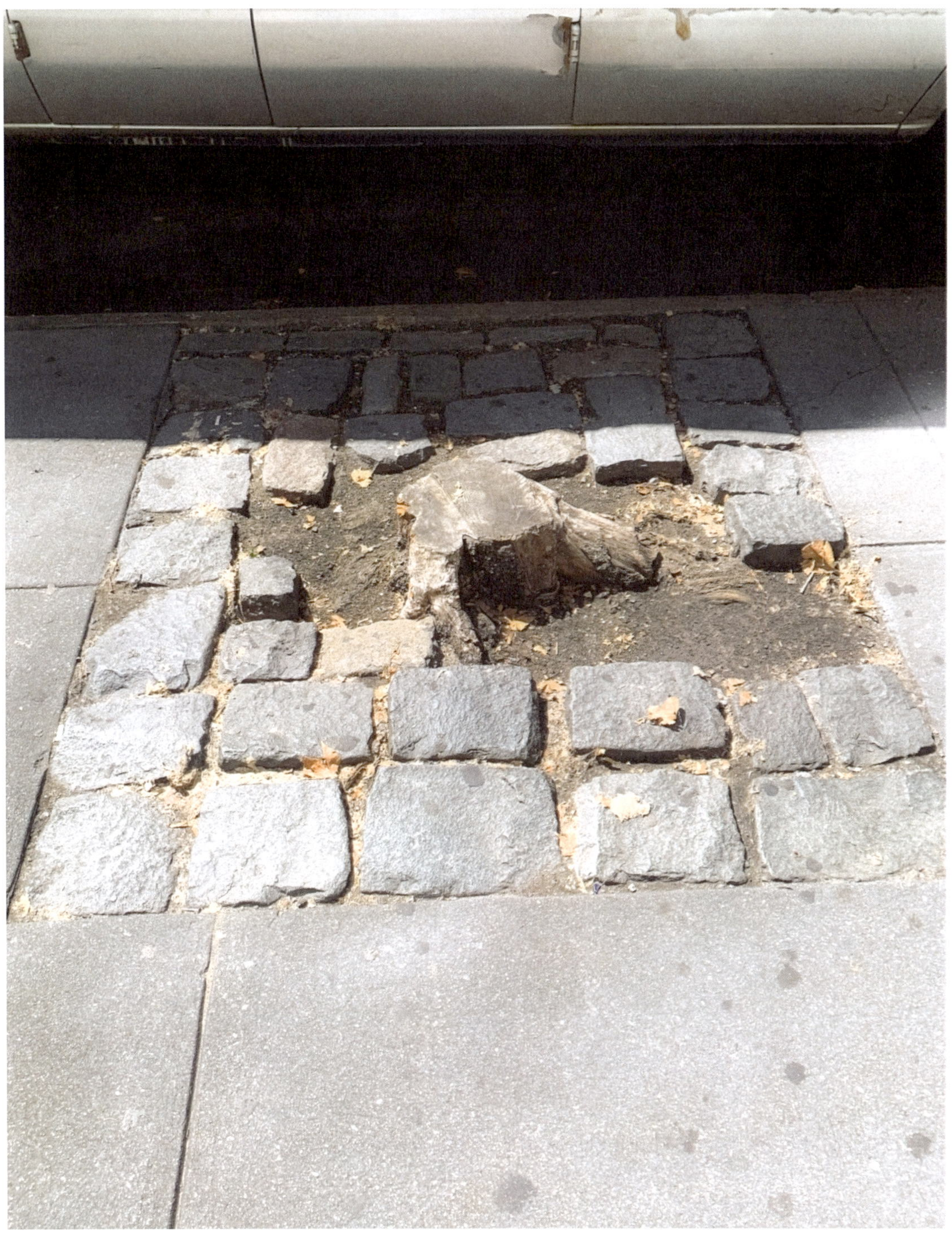

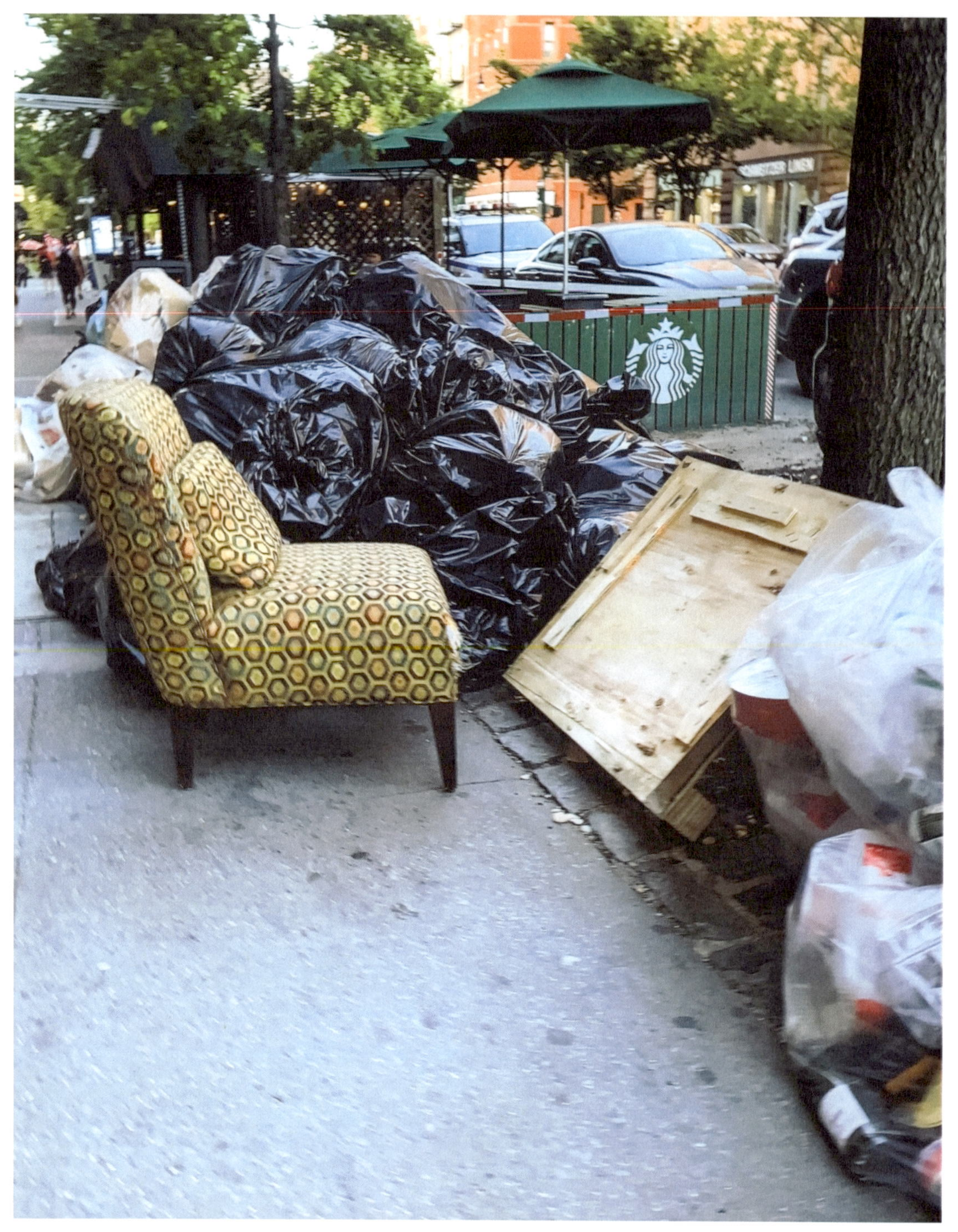

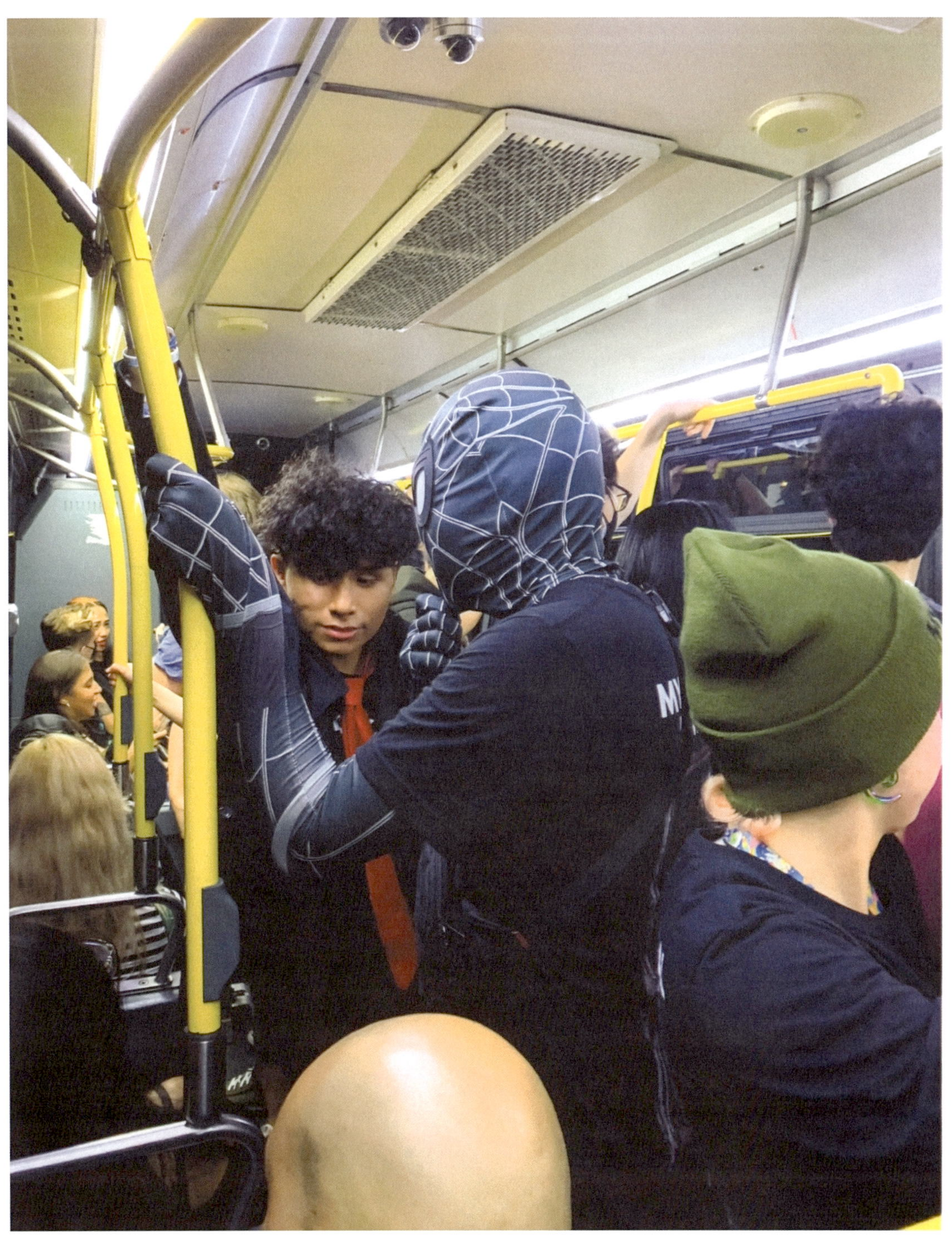

AROINT THEE
FOUL DEMON!
HER
TAD©

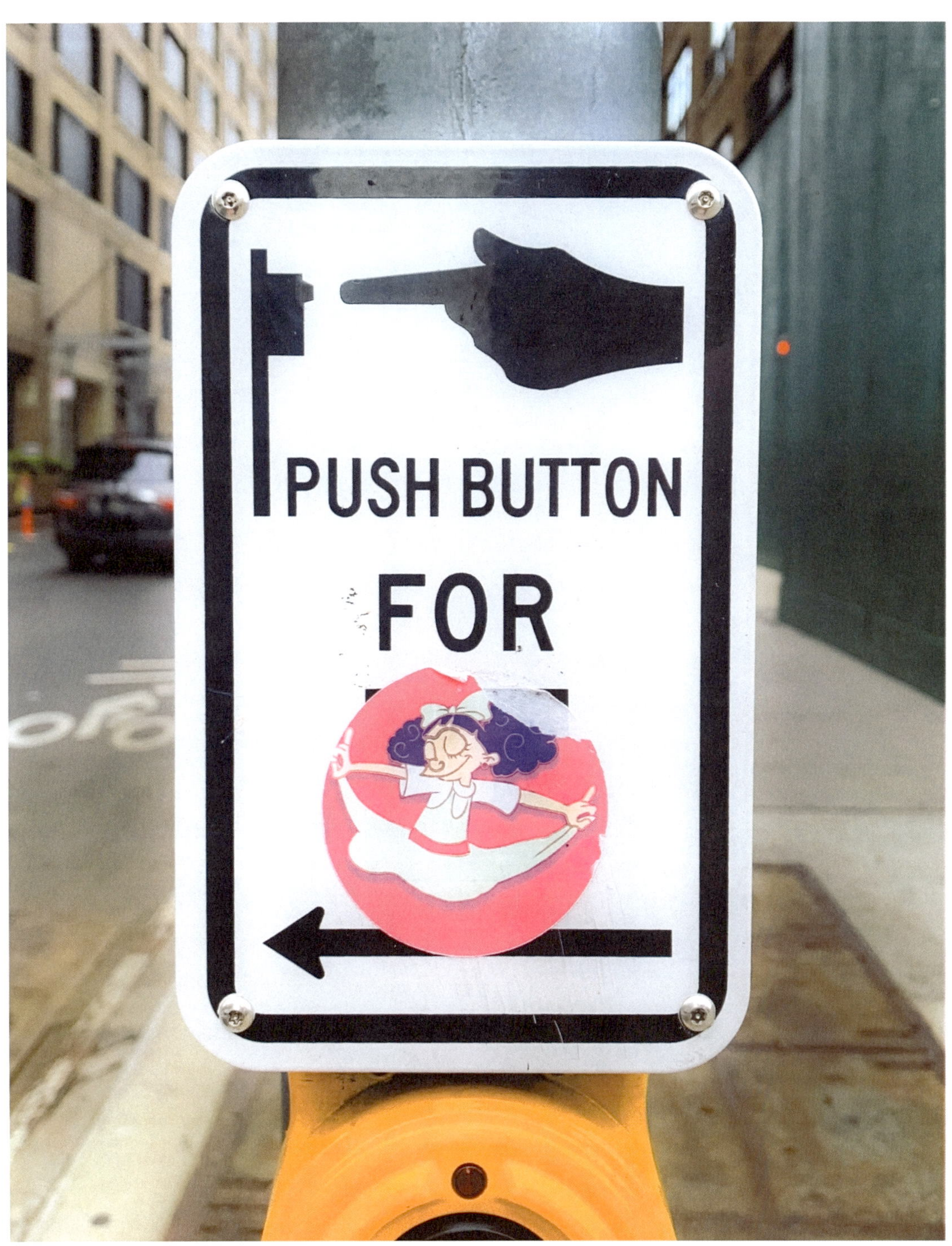

PUSH BUTTON
FOR

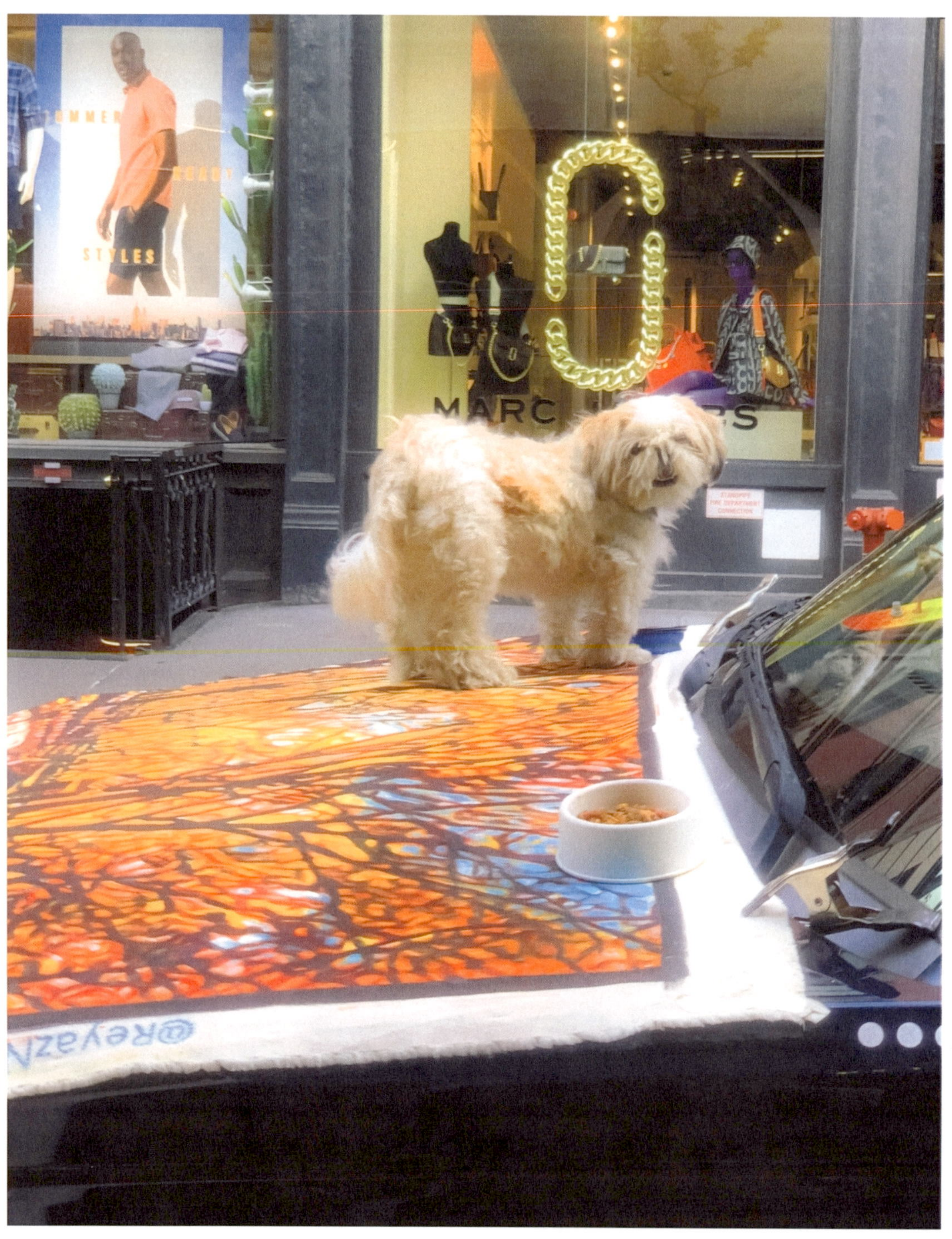
STYLES
MARC   S
STANDPIPE
FIRE DEPARTMENT
CONNECTION
@Reyaz

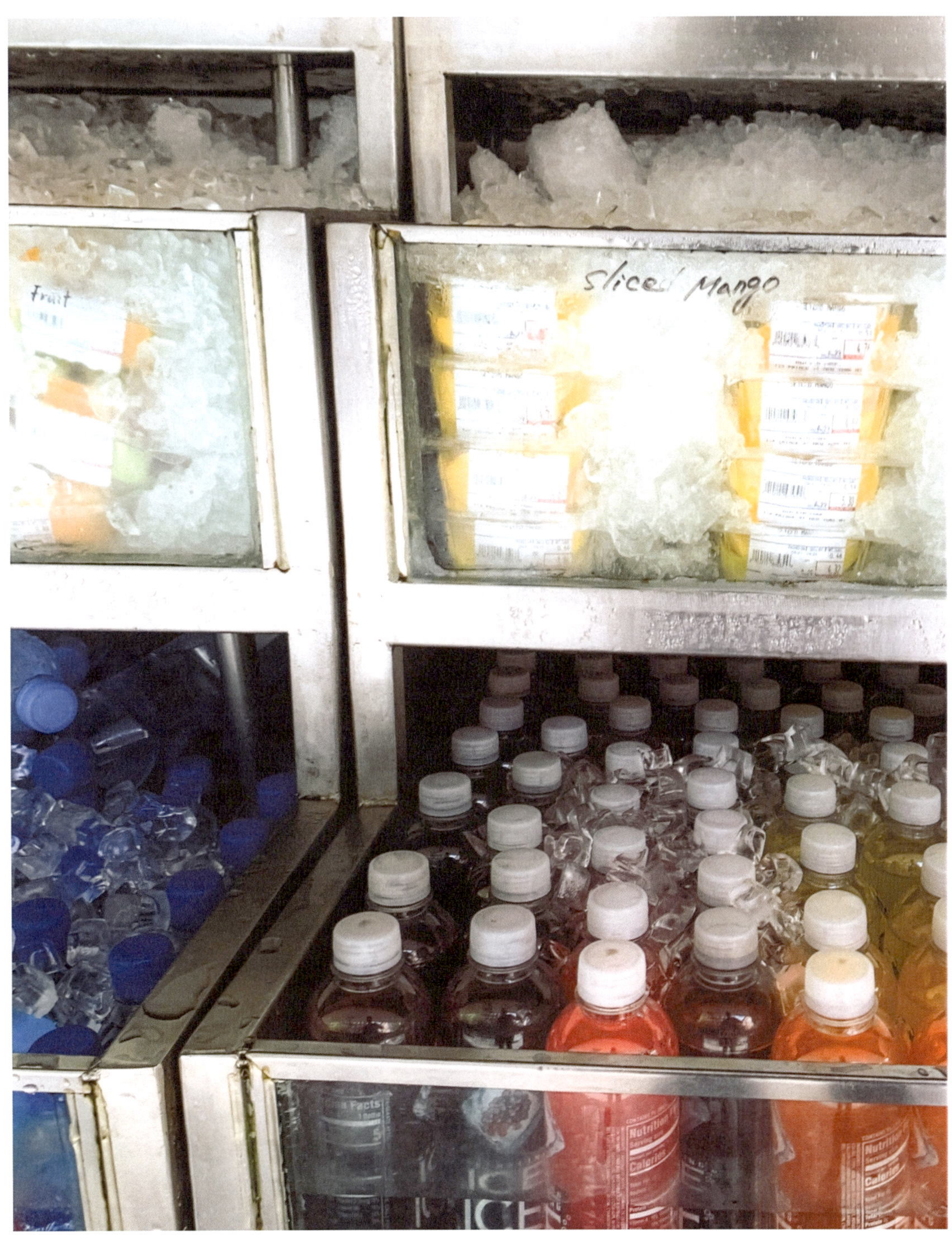

Fruit
sliced Mango

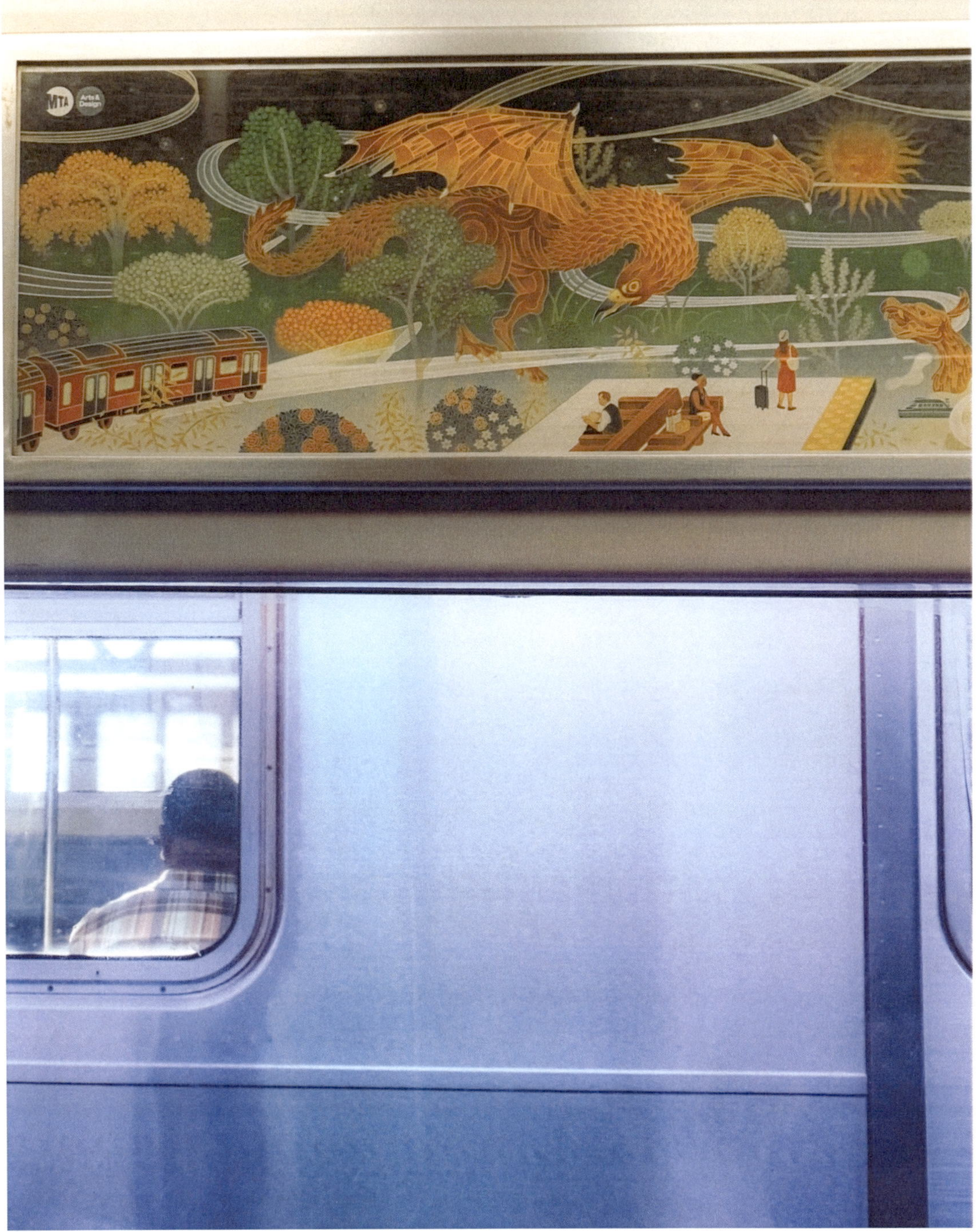

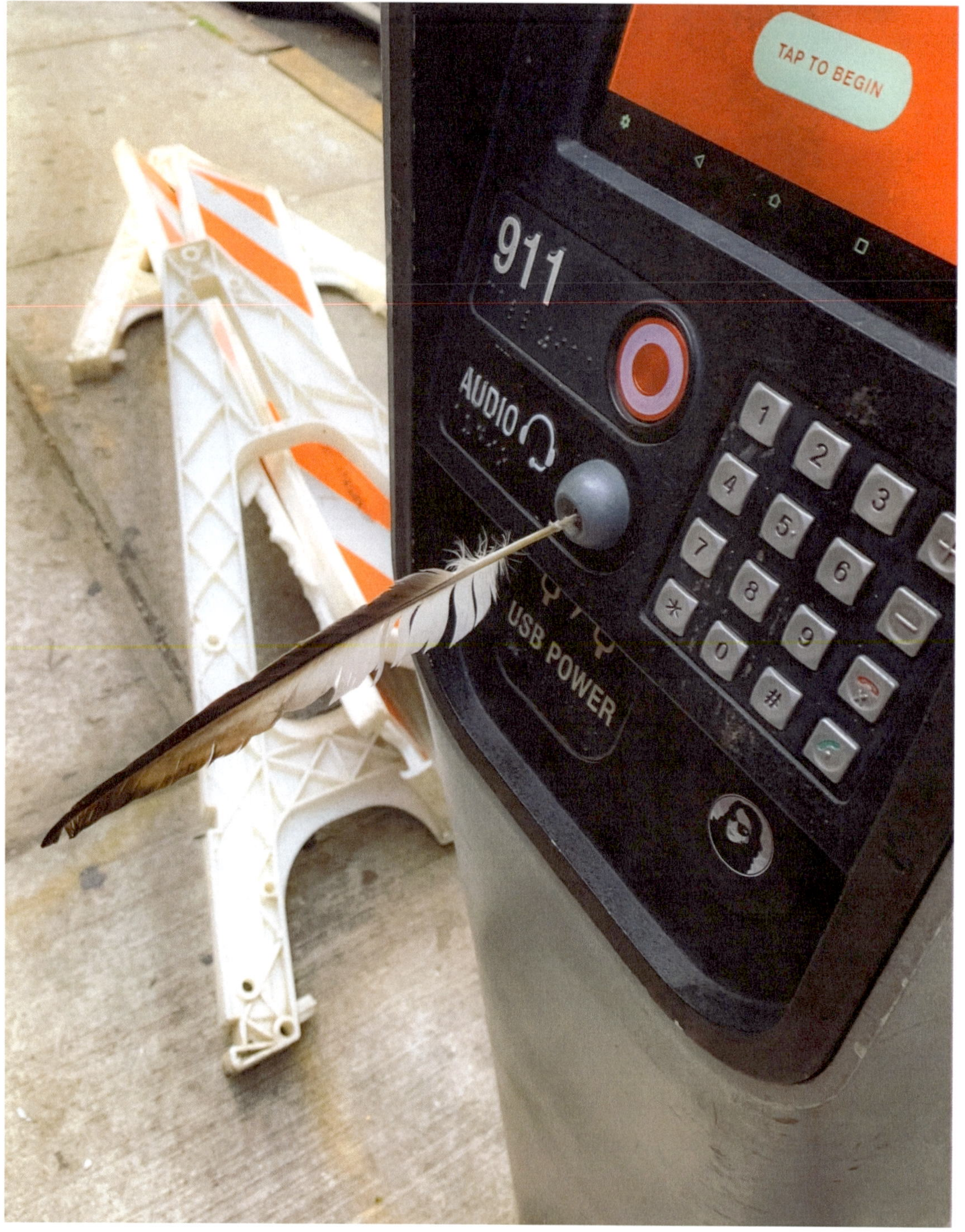

TAP TO BEGIN
911
AUDIO
USB POWER
1
2
3
4
5
6
7
8
9
*
0
#

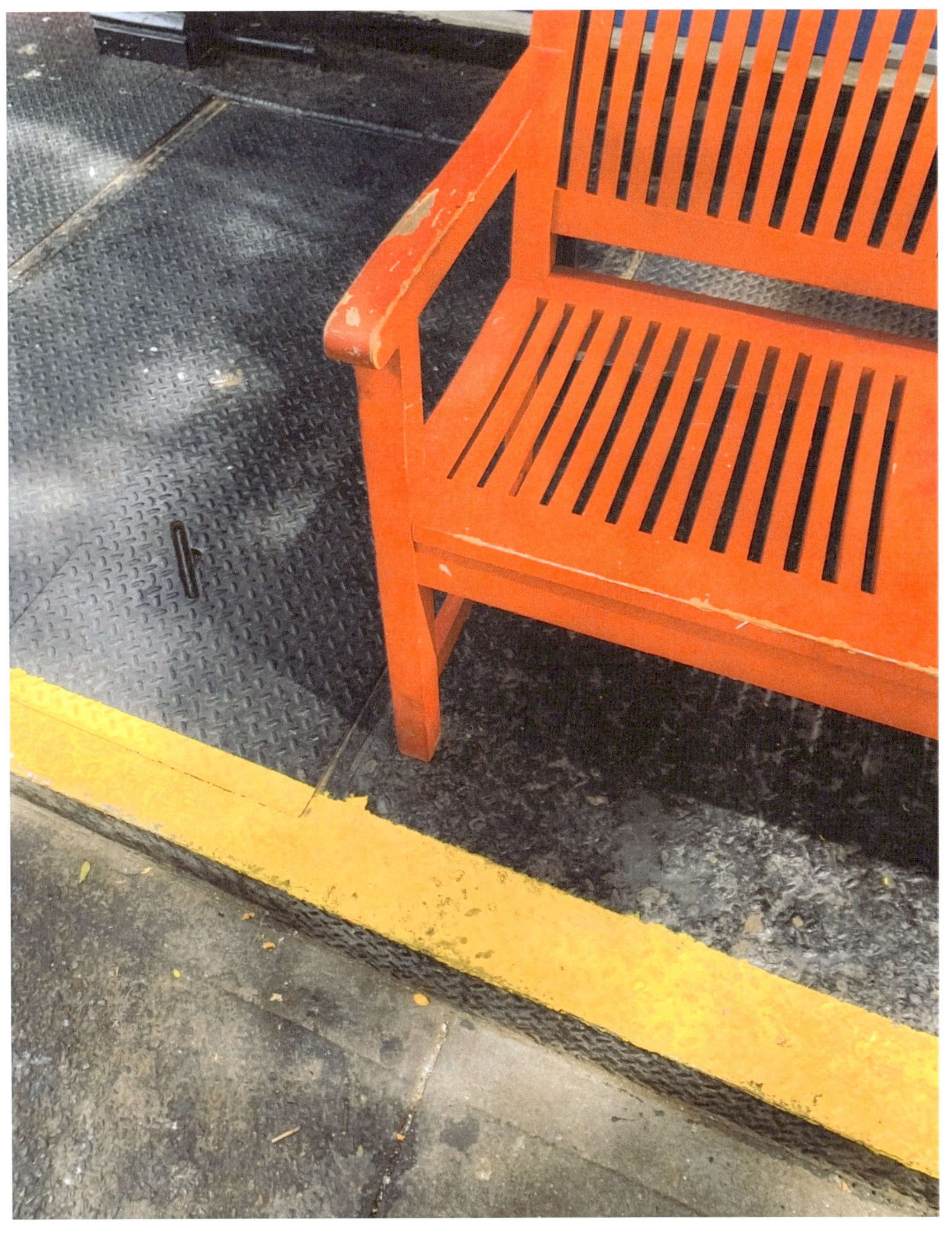

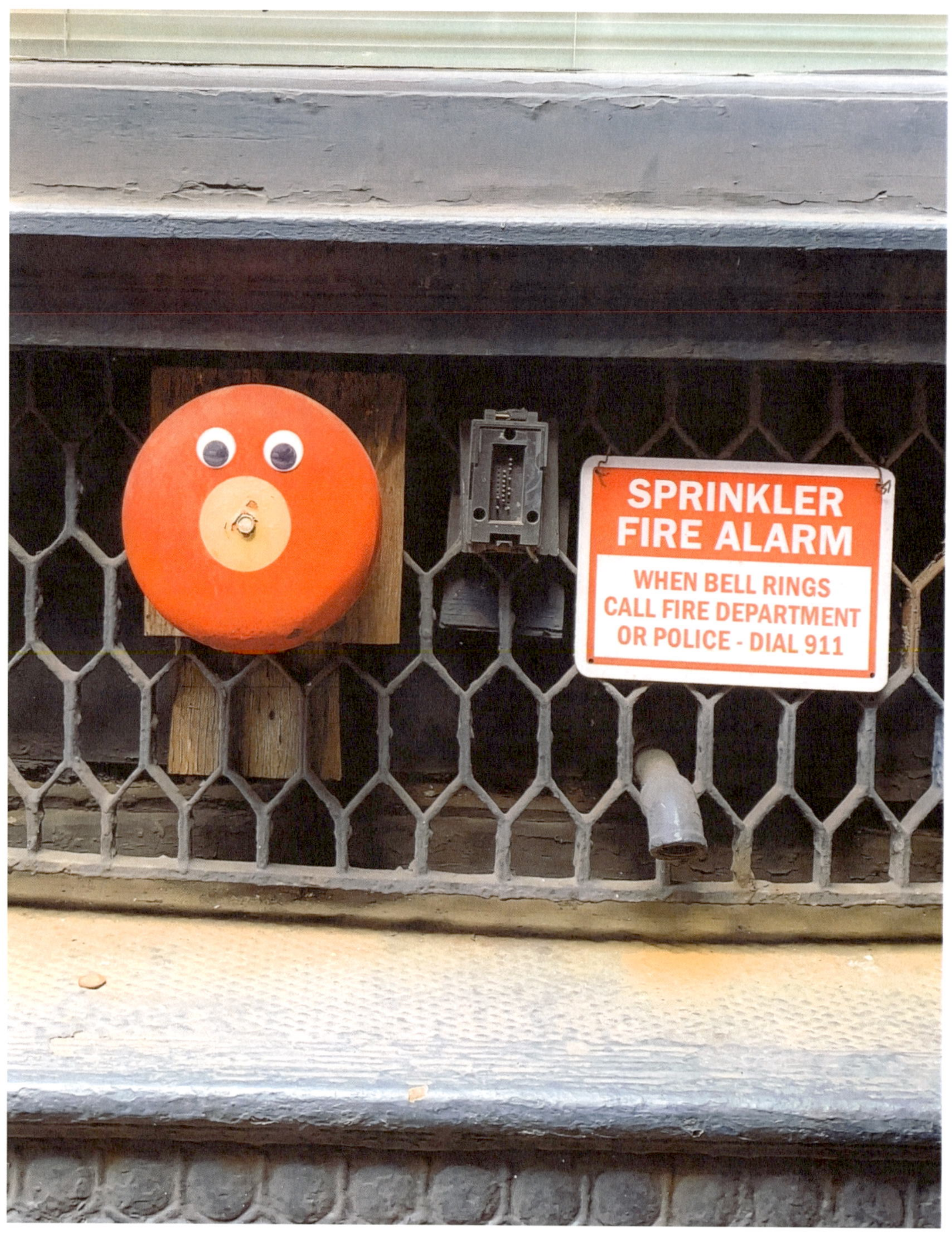

SPRINKLER
FIRE ALARM
WHEN BELL RINGS
CALL FIRE DEPARTMENT
OR POLICE - DIAL 911

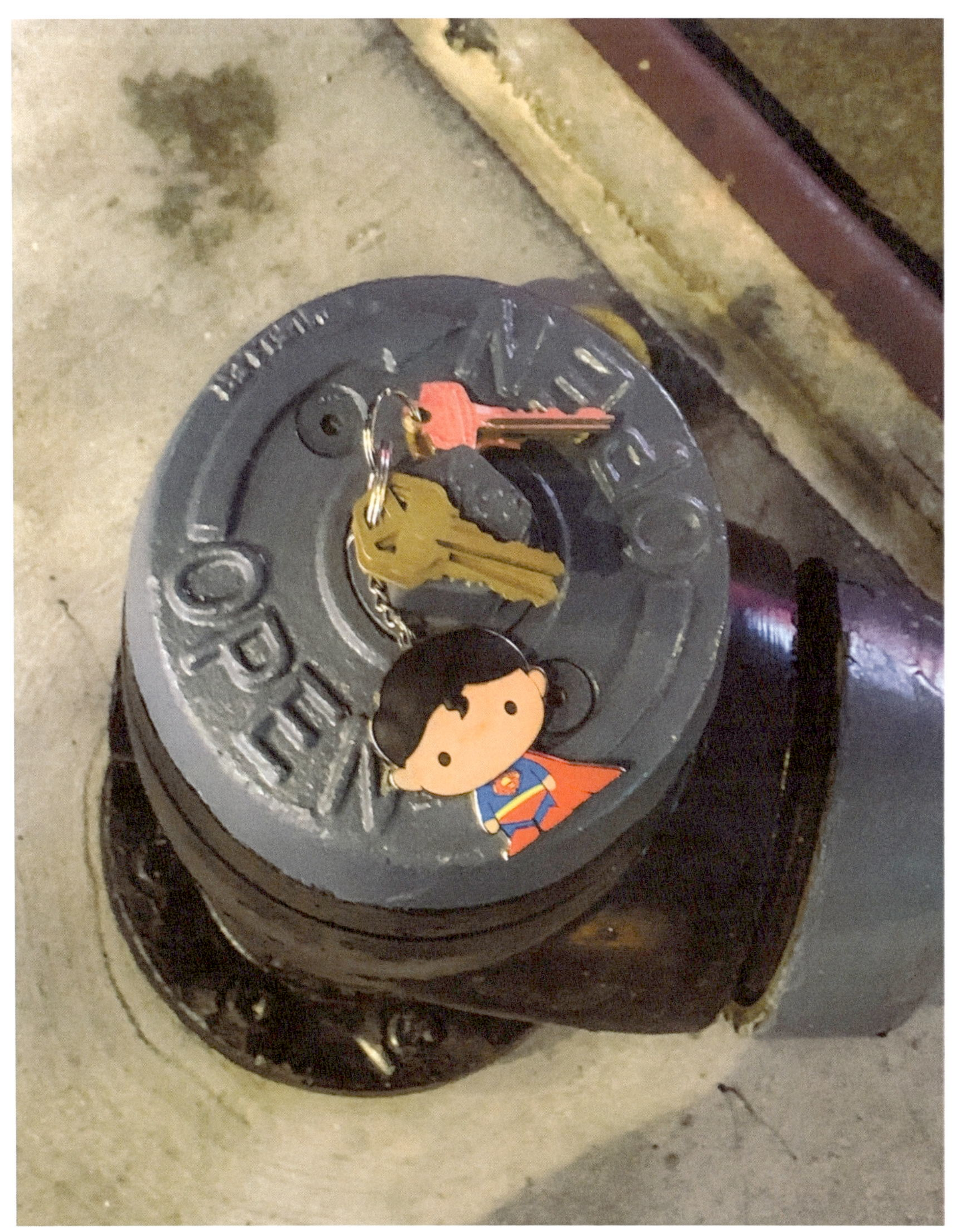

OPEN

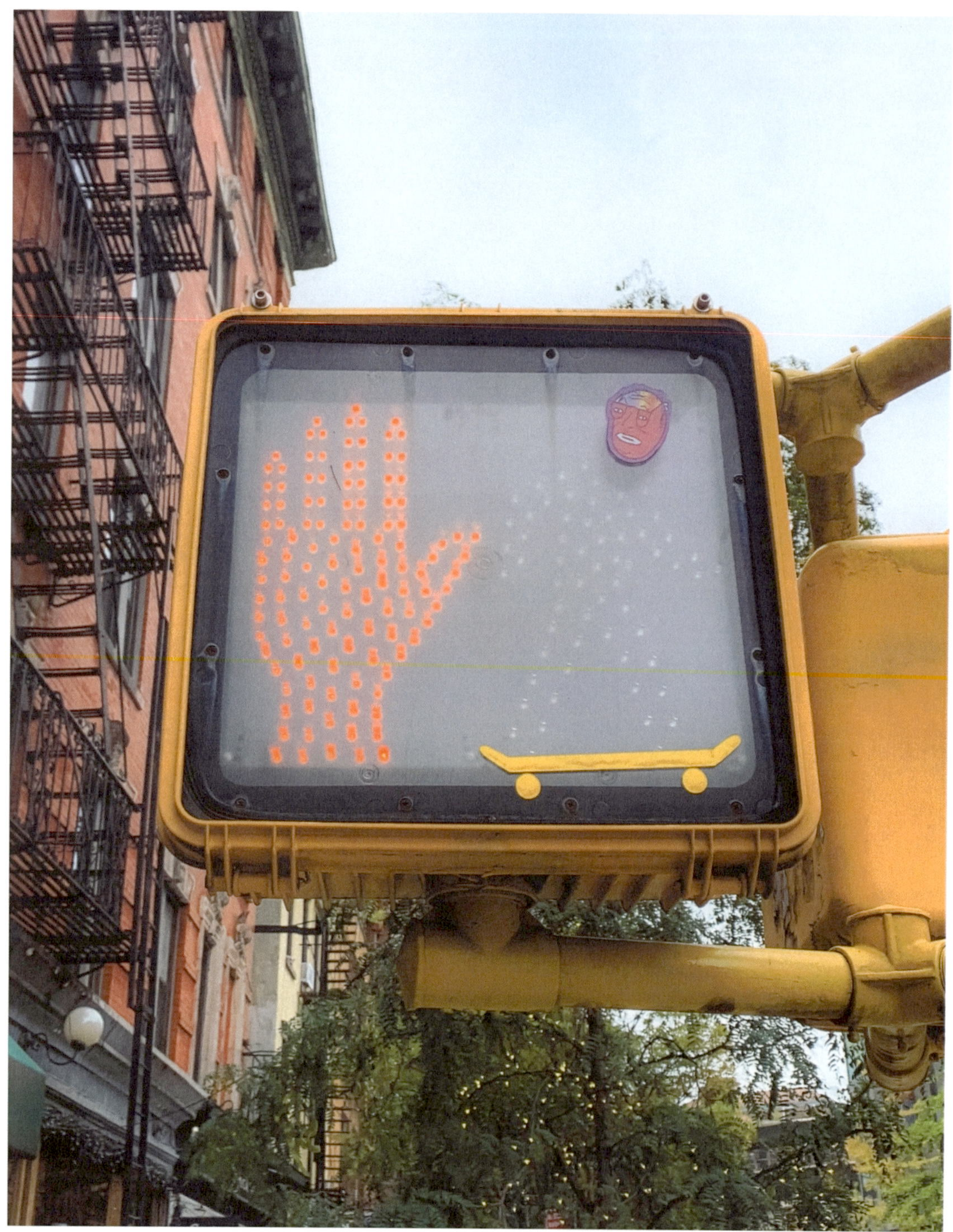

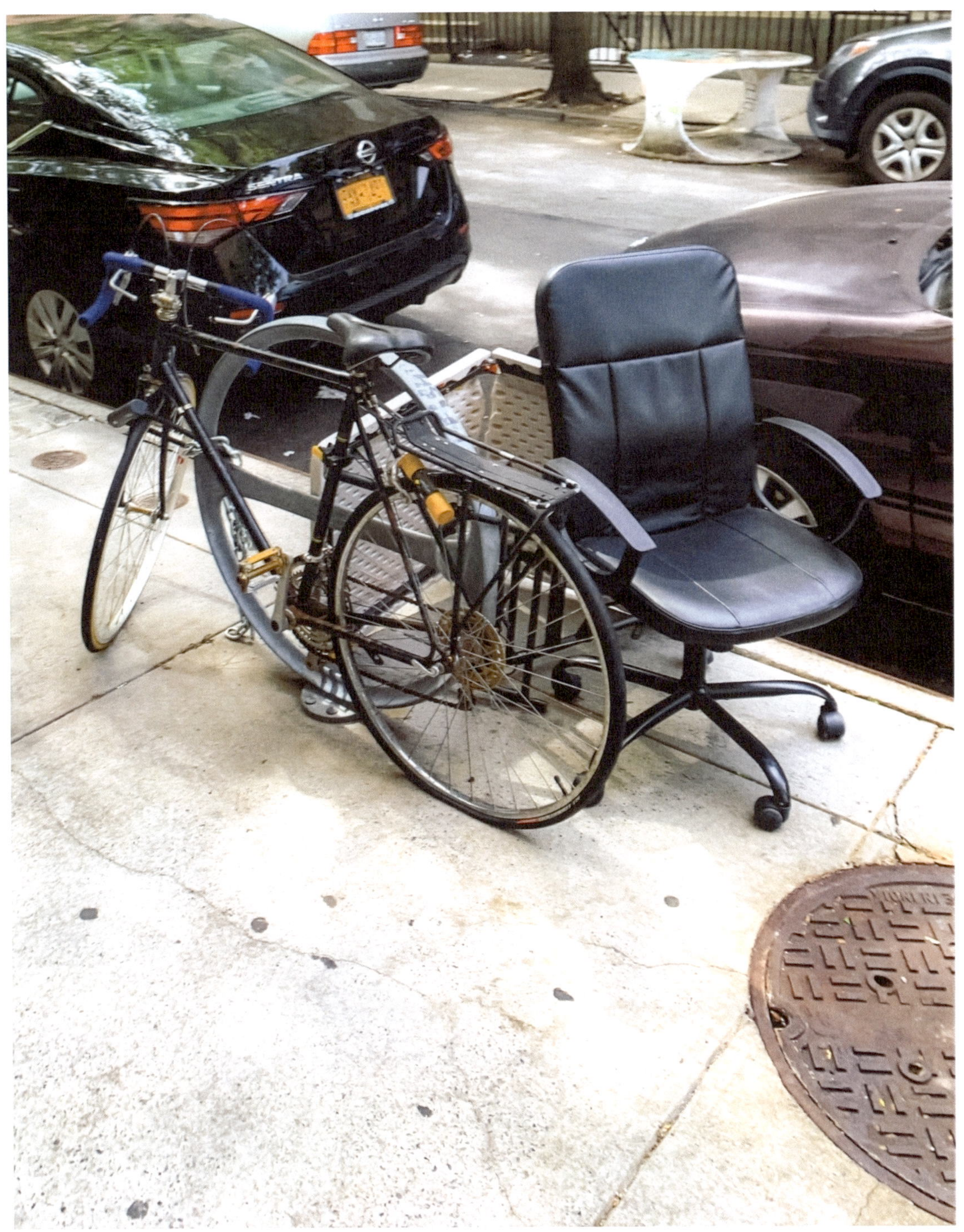

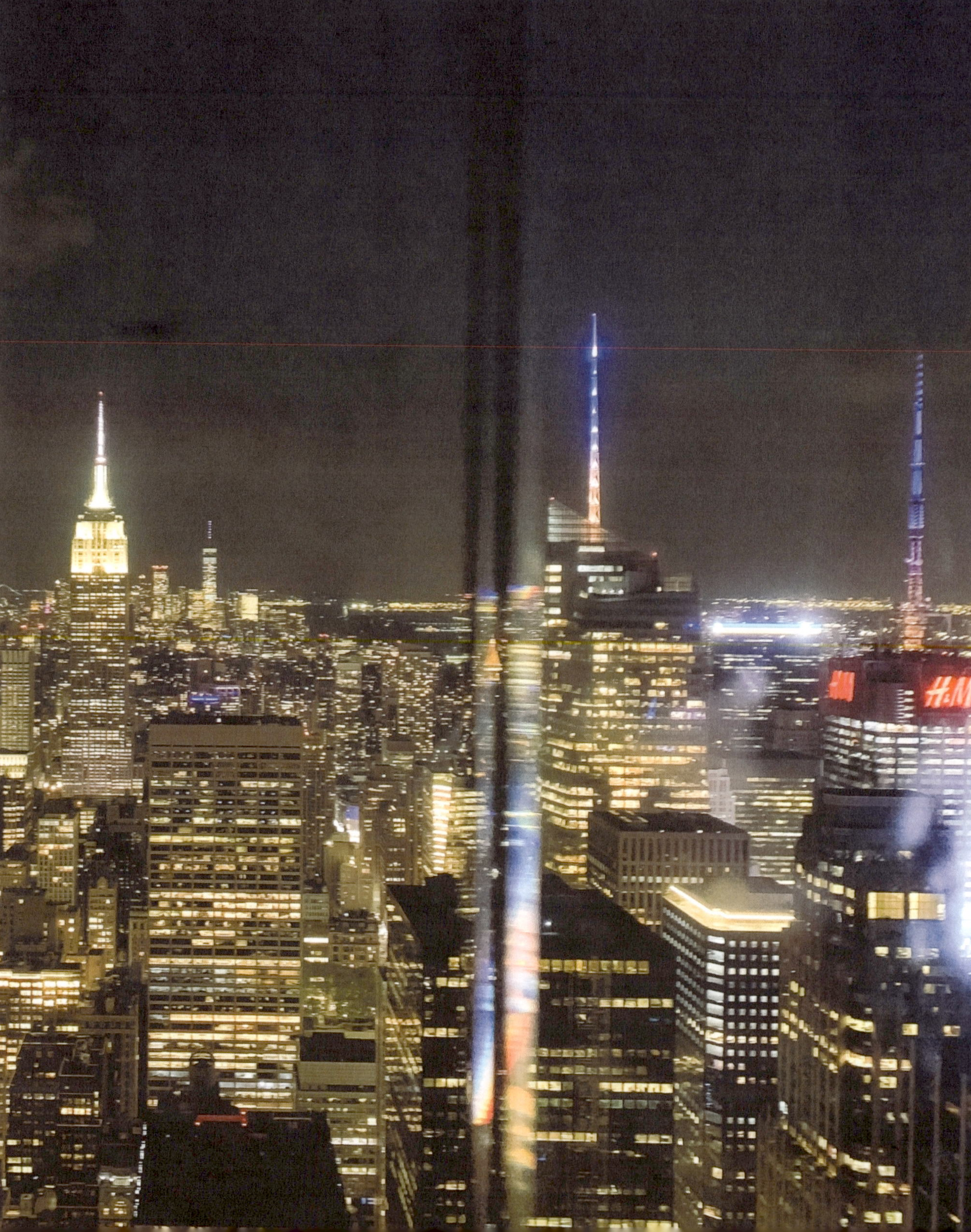

9 781971 080024